The Life of John Bunyan

The Life of John Bunyan

J. Edmund Venables

Cedar Lake Classics

Copyright © 2023 by Cedar Lake Classics

This is a proofread and newly designed edition of a public domain work.

CONTENTS

Chapter 1	1
Chapter 2	14
Chapter 3	34
Chapter 4	50
Chapter 5	59
Chapter 6	68
Chapter 7	77
Chapter 8	98
Chapter 9	121
ABOUT JOHN BUNYAN	141

Chapter 1

John Bunyan, the author of the book which has probably passed through more editions, had a greater number of readers, and been translated into more languages than any other book in the English tongue, was born in the parish of Elstow, in Bedfordshire, in the latter part of the year 1628, and was baptized in the parish church of the village on the last day of November of that year.

The year of John Bunyan's birth was a momentous one both for the nation and for the Church of England. Charles I., by the extorted assent to the Petition of Right, had begun reluctantly to strip himself of the irresponsible authority he had claimed, and had taken the first step in the struggle between King and Parliament which ended in the House of Commons seating itself in the place of the Sovereign. Wentworth (better known as Lord Strafford) had finally left the Commons, baffled in his nobly-conceived but vain hope of reconciling the monarch and his people, and having accepted a peerage and the promise of the Presidency of the Council of the North, was foreshadowing his policy of "Thorough," which was destined to bring both his own head and that of his weak master to the block.

The Remonstrance of Parliament against the toleration of Roman Catholics and the growth of Arminianism, had been presented to the indignant king, who, wilfully blinded, had replied to it by the promotion to high and lucrative posts in the Church of the very men against whom it was chiefly directed. The most outrageous upholders of the royal prerogative and the irresponsible power of the sovereign, Montagu and Mainwaring, had been presented, the one to the see of Chichester, the other—the impeached and condemned of the Commons—to the rich living Montagu's consecration had vacated. Montaigne, the licenser of Mainwaring's incriminated sermon, was raised to the Archbishopric of York, while Neile and Laud, who were openly named in the Remonstrance as the "troublers of the English Israel," were rewarded respectively with the rich see of Durham and the important and deeply-dyed Puritan diocese of London. Charles was steadily sowing the wind, and destined to reap the whirlwind which was to sweep him from his throne, and involve the monarchy and the Church in the same overthrow.

Three months before Bunyan's birth Buckingham, on the eve of his departure for the beleaguered and famine-stricken city of Rochelle, sanguinely hoping to conclude a peace with the French king beneath its walls, had been struck down by the knife of a fanatic, to the undisguised joy of the majority of the nation, bequeathing a legacy of failure and disgrace in the fall of the Protestant stronghold on which the eyes of Europe had been so long anxiously fixed.

The year was closing gloomily, with ominous forecasts of the coming hurricane, when the babe who was destined to leave so imperishable a name in English literature, first saw the light in an humble cottage in an obscure Bedfordshire village. His father, Thomas Bunyan, though styling himself in his will by the more dignified title of "brazier," was more properly what is known as a "tinker"; "a mender of pots and kettles," according to Bunyan's contemporary biographer, Charles Doe. He was not, however, a mere tramp or vagrant, as travelling tinkers were and usually are still, much less a disreputable sot, a counterpart of Shakespeare's Christopher Sly, but a man with a recognized calling, having a settled home and an acknowledged position in the village community of Elstow.

The family was of long standing there, but had for some generations been going down in the world. Bunyan's grandfather, Thomas Bunyan, as we learn from his still extant will, carried on the occupation of a "petty chapman," or small retail dealer, in his own freehold cottage, which he bequeathed, "with its appurtenances," to his second wife, Ann, to descend, after her death, to her stepson, his namesake, Thomas, and her own son Edward, in equal shares. This cottage, which was probably John Bunyan's birthplace, persistent tradition, confirmed by the testimony of local names, warrants us in placing near the hamlet of Harrowden, a mile to the east of the village of Elstow, at a place long called "Bunyan's End," where two fields are still called by the name of "Bunyans" and "Further Bunyans." This small freehold appears to have been all that remained, at the death of John Bunyan's grandfather, of a property once considerable enough to have given the name of its possessor to the whole locality.

The family of Buingnon, Bunyun, Buniun, Boynon, Bonyon, or Binyan (the name is found spelt in no fewer than thirty-four different ways, of which the now-established form, Bunyan, is almost the least frequent) is one that had established itself in Bedfordshire from very early times. The first place in connection with which the name appears is Pulloxhill, about nine miles from Elstow. In 1199, the year of King John's accession, the Bunyans had approached still nearer to that parish. One William Bunion held land at Wilstead, not more than a mile off. In 1327, the first year of Edward III., one of the same name, probably his descendant, William Boynon, is found actually living at Harrowden, close to the spot which popular tradition names as John Bunyan's birthplace, and was the owner of property there.

We have no further notices of the Bunyans of Elstow till the sixteenth century. We then find them greatly fallen. Their ancestral property seems little by little to have passed into other hands, until in 1542 nothing was left but "a messuage and pightell with the appurtenances, and nine acres of land." This small residue other entries on the Court Rolls show to have been still further diminished by sale. The field already referred to, known as "Bonyon's End," was sold by "Thomas Bonyon, of Elstow, labourer," son of William Bonyon, the said Thomas and his wife being the keepers of a small roadside inn, at which their overcharges for their home-baked bread and home-brewed beer were continually bringing them into trouble with the petty local courts of the day.

Thomas Bunyan, John Bunyan's father, was born in the last days of Elizabeth, and was baptized February 24, 1603, exactly a month before the great queen passed away. The mother of the immortal Dreamer was one Margaret Bentley, who, like her husband, was a native of Elstow and only a few months his junior. The details of her mother's will, which is still extant, drawn up by the vicar of Elstow, prove that, like her husband, she did not, in the words of Bunyan's latest and most complete biographer, the Rev. Dr. Brown, "come of the very squalid poor, but of people who, though humble in station, were yet decent and worthy in their ways."

John Bunyan's mother was his father's second wife. The Bunyans were given to marrying early, and speedily consoled themselves on the loss of one wife with the companionship of a successor. Bunyan's grandmother cannot have died before February 24, 1603, the date of his father's baptism. But before the year was out his grandfather had married again. His father, too, had not completed his twentieth year when he married his first wife, Anne Pinney, January 10, 1623. She died in 1627, apparently without any surviving children, and before the year was half-way through, on the 23rd of the following May, he was married a second time to Margaret Bentley.

At the end of seventeen years Thomas Bunyan was again left a widower, and within two months, with grossly indecent haste, he filled the vacant place with a third wife. Bunyan himself cannot have been much more than twenty when he married. We have no particulars of the death of his first wife. But he had been married two years to his noble-minded second wife at the time of the assizes in 1661, and the ages of his children by his first wife would indicate that no long interval elapsed between his being left a widower and his second marriage.

Elstow, which, as the birthplace of the author of "The Pilgrim's Progress," has gained a world-wide celebrity, is a quiet little village, which, though not much more than a mile from the populous and busy town of Bedford, yet, lying aside from the main stream of modern life, preserves its old-world look to an unusual degree. Its name in its original form of "Helen-stow," or "Ellen-stow," the stow or stockaded place of St. Helena, is derived from a Benedictine nunnery founded in 1078 by Judith, niece of William the Conqueror, the traitorous wife of the judicially murdered Waltheof, Earl of Huntingdon, in honour of the mother of the Emperor Constantine.

The parish church, so intimately connected with Bunyan's personal history, is a fragment of the church of the nunnery, with a detached campanile, or "steeple-house," built to contain the bells after the destruction of the central tower and choir of the conventual church. Few villages are so little modernized as Elstow. The old half-timbered cottages with overhanging storeys, peaked dormers, and gabled porches, tapestried with roses and honeysuckles, must be much what they were in Bunyan's days. A village street, with detached cottages standing in gardens gay with the homely flowers John Bunyan knew and loved, leads to the village green, fringed with churchyard elms, in the middle of which is the pedestal or stump of the market-cross, and at the upper end of the old "Moot Hall," a quaint brick and timber building, with a projecting upper storey, a good example of the domestic architecture of the fifteenth century, originally, perhaps, the Guesten-Hall of the adjacent nunnery, and afterwards the Court House of the manor when lay-lords had succeeded the abbesses—"the scene," writes Dr. Brown "of village festivities, statute hirings, and all the public occasions of village life."

The whole spot and its surroundings can be but little altered from the time when our hero was the ringleader of the youth of the place in the dances on the greensward, which he tells us he found it so hard to give up, and in "tip-cat," and the other innocent games which his diseased conscience afterwards regarded as "ungodly practices." One may almost see the hole from which he was going to strike his "cat" that memorable Sunday afternoon when he silenced the inward voice which rebuked him for his sins, and "returned desperately to his sport again."

On the south side of the green, as we have said, stands the church, a fine though somewhat rude fragment of the chapel of the nunnery curtailed at both ends, of Norman and Early English date, which, with its detached bell tower, was the scene of some of the fierce spiritual conflicts so vividly depicted by Bunyan in his "Grace Abounding." On entering every object speaks of Bunyan. The pulpit—if it has survived the recent restoration—is the same from which Christopher Hall, the then "Parson" of Elstow, preached the sermon which first awoke his sleeping conscience.

The font is that in which he was baptized, as were also his father and mother and remoter progenitors, as well as his children, Mary, his dearly-loved blind child, on July 20, 1650, and her younger sister, Elizabeth, on April 14, 1654. An old oaken bench, polished by the hands of thousands of visitors attracted to the village church by the fame of the tinker of Elstow, is traditionally shown as the seat he used to occupy when he "went to church twice a day, and that, too, with the foremost counting all things holy that were therein contained." The five bells which hang in the belfry are the same in which Bunyan so much delighted, the fourth bell, tradition says, being that he was used to ring.

The rough flagged floor, "all worn and broken with the hobnailed boots of generations of ringers," remains undisturbed. One cannot see the door, set in its solid masonry, without recalling the figure of Bunyan standing in it, after conscience, "beginning to be tender," told him that "such practice was but vain," but yet unable to deny himself the pleasure of seeing others ring, hoping that, "if a bell should fall," he could "slip out" safely "behind the thick walls," and so "be preserved notwithstanding." Behind the church, on the south side, stand some picturesque ivy-clad remains of the once stately mansion of the Hillersdons, erected on the site of the nunnery buildings in the early part of the seventeenth century, with a porch attributed to Inigo Jones, which may have given Bunyan the first idea of "the very stately Palace, the name of which was Beautiful."

The cottage where Bunyan was born, between the two brooks in the fields at Harrowden, has been so long destroyed that even the knowledge of its site has passed away. That in which he lived for six years (1649-1655) after his first marriage, and where his children were born, is still standing in the village street, but modern reparations have robbed it of all interest.

From this description of the surroundings among which Bunyan passed the earliest and most impressionable years of his life, we pass to the subject of our biography himself. The notion that Bunyan was of gipsy descent, which was not entirely rejected by Sir Walter Scott, and which has more recently received elaborate support from writers on the other side of the Atlantic, may be pronounced absolutely baseless.

Even if Bunyan's inquiry of his father "whether the family was of Israelitish descent or no," which has been so strangely pressed into the service of the theory, could be supposed to have anything to do with the matter, the decided negative with which his question was met—"he told me, 'No, we were not'"—would, one would have thought, have settled the point. But some fictions die hard. However low the family had sunk, so that in his own words, "his father's house was of that rank that is meanest and most despised of all the families in the land," "of a low and inconsiderable generation," the name, as we have seen, was one of long standing in Bunyan's native county, and had once taken far higher rank in it.

And his parents, though poor, were evidently worthy people, of good repute among their village neighbours. Bunyan seems to be describing his own father and his wandering life when he speaks of "an honest poor labouring man, who, like Adam unparadised, had all the world to get his bread in, and was very careful to maintain his family." He and his wife were also careful with a higher care that their children should be properly educated. "Notwithstanding the meanness and inconsiderableness of my parents," writes Bunyan, "it pleased God to put it into their hearts to put me to school, to learn both to read and write."

If we accept the evidence of the "Scriptural Poems," published for the first time twelve years after his death, the genuineness of which, though questioned by Dr. Brown, there seems no sufficient reason to doubt, the little education he had was "gained in a grammar school." This would have been that founded by Sir William Harpur in Queen Mary's reign in the neighbouring town of Bedford. Thither we may picture the little lad trudging day by day along the mile and a half of footpath and road from his father's cottage by the brookside, often, no doubt, wet and miry enough, not, as he says, to "go to school to Aristotle or Plato," but to be taught "according to the rate of other poor men's children." The Bedford schoolmaster about this time, William Barnes by name, was a negligent sot, charged with "night-walking" and haunting "taverns and alehouses," and other evil practices, as well as with treating the poor boys "when present" with a cruelty which must have made them wish that his absences, long as they were, had been more protracted.

Whether this man was his master or no, it was little that Bunyan learnt at school, and that little he confesses with shame he soon lost "almost utterly." He was before long called home to help his father at the Harrowden forge, where he says he was "brought up in a very mean condition among a company of poor countrymen." Here, with but little to elevate or refine his character, the boy contracted many bad habits, and grew up what Coleridge somewhat too strongly calls "a bitter blackguard."

According to his own remorseful confession, he was "filled with all unrighteousness," having "from a child" in his "tender years," "but few equals both for cursing, swearing, lying and blaspheming the holy name of God." Sins of this kind he declares became "a second nature to him;" he "delighted in all transgression against the law of God," and as he advanced in his teens he became a "notorious sinbreeder," the "very ringleader," he says, of the village lads "in all manner of vice and ungodliness." But the unsparing condemnation passed by Bunyan, after his conversion, on his former self, must not mislead us into supposing him ever, either as boy or man, to have lived a vicious life. "The wickedness of the tinker," writes Southey, "has been greatly overrated, and it is taking the language of self-accusation too literally to pronounce of John Bunyan that he was at any time depraved."

The justice of this verdict of acquittal is fully accepted by Coleridge. "Bunyan," he says, "was never in our received sense of the word 'wicked.'

He was chaste, sober, and honest." He hints at youthful escapades, such, perhaps, as orchard-robbing, or when a little older, poaching, and the like, which might have brought him under "the stroke of the laws," and put him to "open shame before the face of the world." But he confesses to no crime or profligate habit. We have no reason to suppose that he was ever drunk, and we have his own most solemn declaration that he was never guilty of an act of unchastity. "In our days," to quote Mr. Froude, "a rough tinker who could say as much for himself after he had grown to manhood, would be regarded as a model of self-restraint. If in Bedford and the neighbourhood there was no young man more vicious than Bunyan, the moral standard of an English town in the seventeenth century must have been higher than believers in progress will be pleased to allow." How then, it may be asked, are we to explain the passionate language in which he expresses his self-abhorrence, which would hardly seem exaggerated in the mouth of the most profligate and licentious?

We are confident that Bunyan meant what he said. So intensely honest a nature could not allow his words to go beyond his convictions. When he speaks of "letting loose the reins to his lusts," and sinning "with the greatest delight and ease," we know that however exaggerated they may appear to us, his expressions did not seem to him overstrained. Dr. Johnson marvelled that St. Paul could call himself "the chief of sinners," and expressed a doubt whether he did so honestly. But a highly-strung spiritual nature like that of the apostle, when suddenly called into exercise after a period of carelessness, takes a very different estimate of sin from that of the world, even the decent moral world, in general. It realizes its own offences, venial as they appear to others, as sins against infinite love—a love unto death—and in the light of the sacrifice on Calvary, recognizes the heinousness of its guilt, and while it doubts not, marvels that it can be pardoned.

The sinfulness of sin—more especially their own sin—is the intensest of all possible realities to them. No language is too strong to describe it. We may not unreasonably ask whether this estimate, however exaggerated it may appear to those who are strangers to these spiritual experiences, is altogether a mistaken one?

The spiritual instinct was very early awakened in Bunyan. While still a child "but nine or ten years old," he tells us he was racked with convictions of sin, and haunted with religious fears. He was scared with "fearful dreams," and "dreadful visions," and haunted in his sleep with "apprehensions of devils and wicked spirits" coming to carry him away, which made his bed a place of terrors. The thought of the Day of Judgment and of the torments of the lost, often came as a dark cloud over his mind in the midst of his boyish sports, and made him tremble.

But though these fevered visions embittered his enjoyment while they lasted, they were but transient, and after a while they entirely ceased "as if they had never been," and he gave himself up without restraint to the youthful pleasures in which his ardent nature made him ever the ringleader. The "thoughts of religion" became very grievous to him. He could not endure even to see others read pious books; "it would be as a prison to me." The awful realities of eternity which had once been so crushing to his spirit were "both out of sight and mind." He said to God, "depart from me." According to the later morbid estimate which stigmatized as sinful what were little more than the wild acts of a roystering dare-devil young fellow, full of animal spirits and with an unusually active imagination, he "could sin with the greatest delight and ease, and take pleasure in the vileness of his companions." But that the sense of religion was not wholly dead in him even then, and that while discarding its restraints he had an inward reverence for it, is shown by the horror he experienced if those who had a reputation for godliness dishonoured their profession. "Once," he says, "when I was at the height of my vanity, hearing one to swear who was reckoned for a religious man, it had so great a stroke upon my spirit that it made my heart to ache."

This undercurrent of religious feeling was deepened by providential escapes from accidents which threatened his life—"judgments mixed with mercy" he terms them,—which made him feel that he was not utterly forsaken of God. Twice he narrowly escaped drowning; once in "Bedford river"—the Ouse; once in "a creek of the sea," his tinkering rounds having, perhaps, carried him as far northward as the tidal inlets of the Wash in the neighbourhood of Spalding or Lynn, or to the estuaries of the Stour and Orwell to the east. At another time, in his wild contempt of danger, he tore out, while his companions looked on with admiration, what he mistakenly supposed to be an adder's sting.

These providential deliverances bring us to that incident in his brief career as a soldier which his anonymous biographer tells us "made so deep an impression upon him that he would never mention it, which he often did, without thanksgiving to God." But for this occurrence, indeed, we should have probably never known that he had ever served in the army at all. The story is best told in his own provokingly brief words—"When I was a soldier I with others were drawn out to go to such a place to besiege it.

But when I was just ready to go, one of the company desired to go in my room; to which when I consented, he took my place, and coming to the siege, as he stood sentinel, he was shot in the head with a musket bullet and died." Here, as is so often the case in Bunyan's autobiography, we have reason to lament the complete absence of details. This is characteristic of the man. The religious import of the occurrences he records constituted their only value in his eyes; their temporal setting, which imparts their chief interest to us, was of no account to him. He gives us not the slightest clue to the name of the besieged place, or even to the side on which he was engaged. The date of the event is left equally vague. The last point however we are able to determine with something like accuracy. November, 1644, was the earliest period at which Bunyan could have entered the army, for it was not till then that he reached the regulation age of sixteen.

Domestic circumstances had then recently occurred which may have tended to estrange him from his home, and turn his thoughts to a military life. In the previous June his mother had died, her death being followed within a month by that of his sister Margaret. Before another month was out, his father, as we have already said, had married again, and whether the new wife had proved the proverbial injusta noverca or not, his home must have been sufficiently altered by the double, if we may not say triple, calamity, to account for his leaving the dull monotony of his native village for the more stirring career of a soldier. Which of the two causes then distracting the nation claimed his adherence, Royalist or Parliamentarian, can never be determined.

As Mr. Froude writes, "He does not tell us himself. His friends in after life did not care to ask him or he to inform them, or else they thought the matter of too small importance to be worth mentioning with exactness." The only evidence is internal, and the deductions from it vary with the estimate of the counter-balancing probabilities taken by Bunyan's various biographers. Lord Macaulay, whose conclusion is ably, and, we think, convincingly supported by Dr. Brown, decides in favour of the side of the Parliament.

Mr. Froude, on the other hand, together with the painstaking Mr. Offor, holds that "probability is on the side of his having been with the Royalists." Bedfordshire, however, was one of the "Associated Counties" from which the Parliamentary army drew its main strength, and it was shut in by a strong line of defence from any combination with the Royalist army. In 1643 the county had received an order requiring it to furnish "able and armed men" to the garrison at Newport Pagnel, which was then the base of operations against the King in that part of England. All probability therefore points to John Bunyan, the lusty young tinker of Elstow, the leader in all manly sports and adventurous enterprises among his mates, and probably caring very little on what side he fought, having been drafted to Newport to serve under Sir Samuel Luke, of Cople, and other Parliamentary commanders.

The place of the siege he refers to is equally undeterminable. A tradition current within a few years of Bunyan's death, which Lord Macaulay rather rashly invests with the certainty of fact, names Leicester. The only direct evidence for this is the statement of an anonymous biographer, who professes to have been a personal friend of Bunyan's, that he was present at the siege of Leicester, in 1645, as a soldier in the Parliamentary army. This statement, however, is in direct defiance of Bunyan's own words. For the one thing certain in the matter is that wherever the siege may have been, Bunyan was not at it. He tells us plainly that he was "drawn to go," and that when he was just starting, he gave up his place to a comrade who went in his room, and was shot through the head. Bunyan's presence at the siege of Leicester, which has been so often reported that it has almost been regarded as an historical truth, must therefore take its place among the baseless creations of a fertile fancy.

Bunyan's military career, wherever passed and under whatever standard, was very short. The civil war was drawing near the end of its first stage when he enlisted. He had only been a soldier a few months when the battle of Naseby, fatal to the royal cause, was fought, June 14, 1645. Bristol was surrendered by Prince Rupert, Sept. 10th. Three days later Montrose was totally defeated at Philiphaugh; and after a vain attempt to relieve Chester, Charles shut himself up in Oxford.

The royal garrisons yielded in quick succession; in 1646 the armies on both sides were disbanded, and the first act in the great national tragedy having come to a close, Bunyan returned to Elstow, and resumed his tinker's work at the paternal forge. His father, old Thomas Bunyan, it may here be mentioned, lived all through his famous son's twelve years' imprisonment, witnessed his growing celebrity as a preacher and a writer, and died in the early part of 1676, just when John Bunyan was passing through his last brief period of durance, which was to give birth to the work which has made him immortal.

Chapter 2

It cannot have been more than two or three years after Bunyan's return home from his short experience of a soldier's life, that he took the step which, more than any other, influences a man's future career for good or for evil. The young tinker married. With his characteristic disregard of all facts or dates but such as concern his spiritual history, Bunyan tells us nothing about the orphan girl he made his wife. Where he found her, who her parents were, where they were married, even her christian name, were all deemed so many irrelevant details. Indeed the fact of his marriage would probably have been passed over altogether but for the important bearing it hid on his inner life. His "mercy," as he calls it, "was to light upon a wife whose father was counted godly," and who, though she brought him no marriage portion, so that they "came together as poor as poor might be," as "poor as howlets," to adopt his own simile, "without so much household stuff as a dish or a spoon betwixt" them, yet brought with her to the Elstow cottage two religious books, which had belonged to her father, and which he "had left her when he died."

These books were "The Plain Man's Pathway to Heaven," the work of Arthur Dent, the puritan incumbent of Shoebury, in Essex—"wearisomely heavy and theologically narrow," writes Dr. Brown—and "The Practise of Piety," by Dr. Lewis Bayley, Bishop of Bangor, and previously chaplain to Prince Henry, which enjoyed a wide reputation with puritans as well as with churchmen. Together with these books, the young wife brought the still more powerful influence of a religious training, and the memory of a holy example, often telling her young graceless husband "what a godly man her father was, and how he would reprove and correct vice both in his house and amongst his neighbours, and what a strict and holy life he lived in his days both in word and deed."

Much as Bunyan tells us he had lost of the "little he had learnt" at school, he had not lost it "utterly." He was still able to read intelligently. His wife's gentle influence prevailed on him to begin "sometimes to read" her father's legacy "with her." This must have been entirely new reading for Bunyan, and certainly at first not much to his taste. What his favourite reading had been up to this time, his own nervous words tell us, "Give me a ballad, a news-book, George on Horseback, or Bevis of Southampton; give me some book that teaches curious arts, that tells of old fables."

But as he and his young wife read these books together at their fireside, a higher taste was gradually awakened in Bunyan's mind; "some things" in them he "found somewhat pleasing" to him, and they "begot" within him "some desires to religion," producing a degree of outward reformation. The spiritual instinct was aroused. He would be a godly man like his wife's father. He began to "go to church twice a day, and that too with the foremost." Nor was it a mere formal attendance, for when there he tells us he took his part with all outward devotion in the service, "both singing and saying as others did; yet," as he penitently confesses, "retaining his wicked life," the wickedness of which, however, did not amount to more than a liking for the sports and games of the lads of the village, bell-ringing, dancing, and the like.

The prohibition of all liturgical forms issued in 1645, the observance of which varied with the strictness or laxity of the local authorities, would not seem to have been put in force very rigidly at Elstow. The vicar, Christopher Hall, was an Episcopalian, who, like Bishop Sanderson, retained his benefice unchallenged all through the Protectorate, and held it some years after the Restoration and the passing of the Act of Uniformity. He seems, like Sanderson, to have kept himself within the letter of the law by making trifling variations in the Prayer Book formularies, consistent with a general conformity to the old order of the Church, "without persisting to his own destruction in the usage of the entire liturgy." The decent dignity of the ceremonial of his parish church had a powerful effect on Bunyan's freshly awakened religious susceptibility—a "spirit of superstition" he called it afterwards—and helped to its fuller development.

"I adored," he says, "with great devotion, even all things, both the High Place"—altars then had not been entirely broken down and levelled in Bedfordshire—"Priest, Clerk, Vestment, Service, and what else belonging to the church, counting all things holy that were therein contained, and especially the Priest and Clerk most happy, and without doubt greatly blessed because they were the servants of God and were principal in the Holy Temple, to do His work therein, . . . their name, their garb, and work, did so intoxicate and bewitch me."

If it is questionable whether the Act forbidding the use of the Book of Common Prayer was strictly observed at Elstow, it is certain that the prohibition of Sunday sports was not. Bunyan's narrative shows that the aspect of a village green in Bedfordshire during the Protectorate did not differ much from what Baxter tells us it had been in Shropshire before the civil troubles began, where, "after the Common Prayer had been read briefly, the rest of the day even till dark night almost, except eating time, was spent in dancing under a maypole and a great tree, when all the town did meet together."

These Sunday sports proved the battle-ground of Bunyan's spiritual experience, the scene of the fierce inward struggles which he has described so vividly, through which he ultimately reached the firm ground of solid peace and hope. As a high-spirited healthy athletic young fellow, all kinds of manly sports were Bunyan's delight. On week days his tinker's business, which he evidently pursued industriously, left him small leisure for such amusements. Sunday therefore was the day on which he "did especially solace himself" with them. He had yet to learn the identification of diversions with "all manner of vice."

The teaching came in this way. One Sunday, Vicar Hall preached a sermon on the sin of Sabbath-breaking, and like many hearers before and since, he imagined that it was aimed expressly at him. Sermon ended, he went home "with a great burden upon his spirit," "sermon-stricken" and "sermon sick" as he expresses it elsewhere. But his Sunday's dinner speedily drove away his self-condemning thoughts. He "shook the sermon out of his mind," and went out to his sports with the Elstow lads on the village green, with as "great delight" as ever. But in the midst of his game of tip-cat or "sly," just as he had struck the "cat" from its hole, and was going to give it a second blow—the minuteness of the detail shows the unforgetable reality of the crisis—he seemed to hear a voice from heaven asking him whether "he would leave his sins and go to heaven, or keep his sins and go to hell." He thought also that he saw Jesus Christ looking down on him with threatening countenance.

But like his own Hopeful he "shut his eyes against the light," and silenced the condemning voice with the feeling that repentance was hopeless. "It was too late for him to look after heaven; he was past pardon." If his condemnation was already sealed and he was eternally lost, it would not matter whether he was condemned for many sins or for few. Heaven was gone already. The only happiness he could look for was what he could get out of his sins—his morbidly sensitive conscience perversely identifying sports with sin—so he returned desperately to his games, resolved, he says, to "take my fill of sin, still studying what sin was yet to be committed that I might taste the sweetness of it."

This desperate recklessness lasted with him "about a month or more," till "one day as he was standing at a neighbour's shop-window, cursing and swearing and playing the madman after his wonted manner, the woman of the house, though a very loose and ungodly wretch," rebuked him so severely as "the ungodliest fellow for swearing that ever she heard, able to spoil all the youth in a whole town," that, self-convicted, he hung down his head in silent shame, wishing himself a little child again that he might unlearn the wicked habit of which he thought it impossible to break himself. Hopeless as the effort seemed to him, it proved effectual. He did "leave off his swearing" to his own "great wonder," and found that he "could speak better and with more pleasantness" than when he "put an oath before and another behind, to give his words authority."

Thus was one step in his reformation taken, and never retraced; but, he adds sorrowfully, "all this while I knew not Jesus Christ, neither did I leave my sports and plays." We might be inclined to ask, why should he leave them? But indifferent and innocent in themselves, an overstrained spirituality had taught him to regard them as sinful. To indulge in them wounded his morbidly sensitive conscience, and so they were sin to him.

The next step onward in this religious progress was the study of the Bible, to which he was led by the conversation of a poor godly neighbour. Naturally he first betook himself to the historical books, which, he tells us, he read "with great pleasure;" but, like Baxter who, beginning his Bible reading in the same course, writes, "I neither understood nor relished much the doctrinal part," he frankly confesses, "Paul's Epistles and such like Scriptures I could not away with." His Bible reading helped forward the outward reformation he had begun. He set the keeping the Ten Commandments before him as his "way to Heaven"; much comforted "sometimes" when, as he thought, "he kept them pretty well," but humbled in conscience when "now and then he broke one."

"But then," he says, "I should repent and say I was sorry for it, and promise God to do better next time, and then get help again; for then I thought I pleased God as well as any man in England." His progress was slow, for each step involved a battle, but it was steadily onwards. He had a very hard struggle in relinquishing his favourite amusements. But though he had much yet to learn, his feet were set on the upward way, and he had no mind to go back, great as the temptation often was. He had once delighted in bell-ringing, but "his conscience beginning to be tender"—morbid we should rather say—"he thought such practise to be vain, and therefore forced himself to leave it."

But "hankering after it still," he continued to go while his old companions rang, and look on at what he "durst not" join in, until the fear that if he thus winked at what his conscience condemned, a bell, or even the tower itself, might fall and kill him, put a stop even to that compromise. Dancing, which from his boyhood he had practised on the village green, or in the old Moot Hall, was still harder to give up. "It was a full year before I could quite leave that." But this too was at last renounced, and finally. The power of Bunyan's indomitable will was bracing itself for severe trials yet to come.

Meanwhile Bunyan's neighbours regarded with amazement the changed life of the profane young tinker. "And truly," he honestly confesses, "so they well might for this my conversion was as great as for Tom of Bedlam to become a sober man." Bunyan's reformation was soon the town's talk; he had "become godly," "become a right honest man." These commendations flattered is vanity, and he laid himself out for them. He was then but a "poor painted hypocrite," he says, "proud of his godliness, and doing all he did either to be seen of, or well spoken of by man." This state of self-satisfaction, he tells us, lasted "for about a twelvemonth or more."

During this deceitful calm he says, "I had great peace of conscience, and should think with myself, 'God cannot choose but now be pleased with me,' yea, to relate it in mine own way, I thought no man in England could please God better than I." But no outward reformation can bring lasting inward peace. When a man is honest with himself, the more earnestly he struggles after complete obedience, the more faulty does his obedience appear. The good opinion of others will not silence his own inward condemnation. He needs a higher righteousness than his own; a firmer standing-ground than the shifting quicksand of his own good deeds. "All this while," he writes, "poor wretch as I was, I was ignorant of Jesus Christ, and going about to establish my own righteousness, and had perished therein had not God in mercy showed me more of my state by nature."

This revolution was nearer than he imagined. Bunyan's self-satisfaction was rudely shaken, and his need of something deeper in the way of religion than he had yet experienced was shown him by the conversation of three or four poor women whom, one day, when pursuing his tinker's calling at Bedford, he came upon "sitting at a door in the sun, and talking of the things of God." These women were members of the congregation of "the holy Mr. John Gifford," who, at that time of ecclesiastical confusion, subsequently became rector of St. John's Church, in Bedford, and master of the hospital attached to it. Gifford's career had been a strange one.

We hear of him first as a young major in the king's army at the outset of the Civil War, notorious for his loose and debauched life, taken by Fairfax at Maidstone in 1648, and condemned to the gallows. By his sister's help he eluded his keepers' vigilance, escaped from prison, and ultimately found his way to Bedford, where for a time he practised as a physician, though without any change of his loose habits. The loss of a large sum of money at gaming awoke a disgust at his dissolute life. A few sentences of a pious book deepened the impression. He became a converted man, and joined himself to a handful of earnest Christians in Bedford, who becoming, in the language of the day, "a church," he was appointed its first minister.

Gifford exercised a deep and vital though narrow influence, leaving behind him at his death, in 1655, the character of a "wise, tolerant, and truly Christian man." The conversation of the poor women who were destined to exercise so momentous an influence on Bunyan's spiritual life, evidenced how thoroughly they had drunk in their pastor's teaching. Bunyan himself was at this time a "brisk talker in the matters of religion," such as he drew from the life in his own Talkative. But the words of these poor women were entirely beyond him. They opened a new and blessed land to which he was a complete stranger. "They spoke of their own wretchedness of heart, of their unbelief, of their miserable state by nature, of the new birth, and the work of God in their souls, and how the Lord refreshed them, and supported them against the temptations of the Devil by His words and promises."

But what seems to have struck Bunyan the most forcibly was the happiness which their religion shed in the hearts of these poor women. Religion up to this time had been to him a system of rules and restrictions. Heaven was to be won by doing certain things and not doing certain other things. Of religion as a Divine life kindled in the soul, and flooding it with a joy which creates a heaven on earth, he had no conception. Joy in believing was a new thing to him. "They spake as if joy did make them speak; they spake with such pleasantness of Scripture language, and with such appearance of grace in all they said, that they were to me as if they had found a new world," a veritable "El Dorado," stored with the true riches.

Bunyan, as he says, after he had listened awhile and wondered at their words, left them and went about his work again. But their words went with him. He could not get rid of them. He saw that though he thought himself a godly man, and his neighbours thought so too, he wanted the true tokens of godliness. He was convinced that godliness was the only true happiness, and he could not rest till he had attained it. So he made it his business to be going again and again into the company of these good women. He could not stay away, and the more he talked with them the more uneasy he became—"the more I questioned my own condition."

The salvation of his soul became all in all to him. His mind "lay fixed on eternity like a horse-leech at the vein." The Bible became precious to him. He read it with new eyes, "as I never did before." "I was indeed then never out of the Bible, either by reading or meditation." The Epistles of St. Paul, which before he "could not away with," were now "sweet and pleasant" to him. He was still "crying out to God that he might know the truth and the way to Heaven and glory." Having no one to guide him in his study of the most difficult of all books, it is no wonder that he misinterpreted and misapplied its words in a manner which went far to unsettle his brain. He read that without faith he could not be saved, and though he did not clearly know what faith was, it became a question of supreme anxiety to him to determine whether he had it or not. If not, he was a castaway indeed, doomed to perish for ever. So he determined to put it to the test.

The Bible told him that faith, "even as a grain of mustard seed," would enable its possessor to work miracles. So, as Mr. Froude says, "not understanding Oriental metaphors," he thought he had here a simple test which would at once solve the question. One day as he was walking along the miry road between Elstow and Bedford, which he had so often paced as a schoolboy, "the temptation came hot upon him" to put the matter to the proof, by saying to the puddles that were in the horse-pads "be dry," and to the dry places, "be ye puddles." He was just about to utter the words when a sudden thought stopped him. Would it not be better just to go under the hedge and pray that God would enable him?

This pause saved him from a rash venture, which might have landed him in despair. For he concluded that if he tried after praying and nothing came of it, it would prove that he had no faith, but was a castaway. "Nay, thought I, if it be so, I will never try yet, but will stay a little longer." "Then," he continues, "I was so tossed betwixt the Devil and my own ignorance, and so perplexed, especially at sometimes, that I could not tell what to do." At another time his mind, as the minds of thousands have been and will be to the end, was greatly harassed by the insoluble problems of predestination and election.

The question was not now whether he had faith, but "whether he was one of the elect or not, and if not, what then?" "He might as well leave off and strive no further." And then the strange fancy occurred to him, that the good people at Bedford whose acquaintance he had recently made, were all that God meant to save in that part of the country, and that the day of grace was past and gone for him; that he had overstood the time of mercy. "Oh that he had turned sooner!" was then his cry. "Oh that he had turned seven years before! What a fool he had been to trifle away his time till his soul and heaven were lost!" The text, "compel them to come in, and yet there is room," came to his rescue when he was so harassed and faint that he was "scarce able to take one step more."

He found them "sweet words," for they showed him that there was "place enough in heaven for him," and he verily believed that when Christ spoke them He was thinking of him, and had them recorded to help him to overcome the vile fear that there was no place left for him in His bosom. But soon another fear succeeded the former. Was he truly called of Christ? "He called to them when He would, and they came to Him." But they could not come unless He called them. Had He called him? Would He call him? If He did how gladly would he run after Him. But oh, he feared that He had no liking to him; that He would not call him. True conversion was what he longed for. "Could it have been gotten for gold," he said, "what could I have given for it! Had I a whole world, it had all gone ten thousand times over for this, that my soul might have been in a converted state." All those whom he thought to be truly converted were now lovely in his eyes. "They shone, they walked like people that carried the broad seal of heaven about them. Oh that he were like them, and shared in their goodly heritage!"

About this time Bunyan was greatly troubled, though at the same time encouraged in his endeavours after the blessedness he longed for so earnestly but could not yet attain to, by "a dream or vision" which presented itself to him, whether in his waking or sleeping hours he does not tell us. He fancied he saw his four Bedford friends refreshing themselves on the sunny side of a high mountain while he was shivering with dark and cold on the other side, parted from them by a high wall with only one small gap in it, and that not found but after long searching, and so strait and narrow withal that it needed long and desperate efforts to force his way through. At last he succeeded. "Then," he says, "I was exceeding glad, and went and sat down in the midst of them, and so was comforted with the light and heat of their sun."

But this sunshine shone but in illusion, and soon gave place to the old sad questioning, which filled his soul with darkness. Was he already called, or should he be called some day? He would give worlds to know. Who could assure him? At last some words of the prophet Joel (chap. iii, 21) encouraged him to hope that if not converted already, the time might come when he should be converted to Christ. Despair began to give way to hopefulness.

At this crisis Bunyan took the step which he would have been wise if he had taken long before. He sought the sympathy and counsel of others. He began to speak his mind to the poor people in Bedford whose words of religious experiences had first revealed to him his true condition. By them he was introduced to their pastor, "the godly Mr. Gifford," who invited him to his house and gave him spiritual counsel. He began to attend the meetings of his disciples.

The teaching he received here was but ill-suited for one of Bunyan's morbid sensitiveness. For it was based upon a constant introspection and a scrupulous weighing of each word and action, with a torturing suspicion of its motive, which made a man's ever-varying spiritual feelings the standard of his state before God, instead of leading him off from self to the Saviour. It is not, therefore, at all surprising that a considerable period intervened before, in the language of his school, "he found peace." This period, which seems to have embraced two or three years, was marked by that tremendous inward struggle which he has described, "as with a pen of fire," in that marvellous piece of religious autobiography, without a counterpart except in "The Confessions of St. Augustine," his "Grace Abounding to the Chief of Sinners." Bunyan's first experiences after his introduction to Mr. Gifford and the inner circle of his disciples were most discouraging.

What he heard of God's dealings with their souls showed him something of "the vanity and inward wretchedness of his wicked heart," and at the same time roused all its hostility to God's will. "It did work at that rate for wickedness as it never did before." "The Canaanites would dwell in the land." "His heart hankered after every foolish vanity, and hung back both to and in every duty, as a clog on the leg of a bird to hinder her from flying." He thought that he was growing "worse and worse," and was "further from conversion than ever before." Though he longed to let Christ into his heart, "his unbelief would, as it were, set its shoulder to the door to keep Him out."

Yet all the while he was tormented with the most perverse scrupulosity of conscience. "As to the act of sinning, I never was more tender than now; I durst not take a pin or a stick, though but so big as a straw, for my conscience now was sore, and would smart at every twist. I could not now tell how to speak my words, for fear I should misplace them. Oh! how gingerly did I then go in all I did or said: I found myself in a miry bog, that shook if I did but stir, and was as those left both of God, and Christ, and the Spirit, and all good things."

All the misdoings of his earlier years rose up against him. There they were, and he could not rid himself of them. He thought that no one could be so bad as he was; "not even the Devil could be his equal: he was more loathsome in his own eyes than a toad." What then must God think of him? Despair seized fast hold of him. He thought he was "forsaken of God and given up to the Devil, and to a reprobate mind." Nor was this a transient fit of despondency. "Thus," he writes, "I continued a long while, even for some years together."

This is not the place minutely to pursue Bunyan's religious history through the sudden alternations of hopes and fears, the fierce temptations, the torturing illusions, the strange perversions of isolated scraps of Bible language—texts torn from their context—the harassing doubts as to the truth of Christianity, the depths of despair and the elevations of joy, which he has portrayed with his own inimitable graphic power. It is a picture of fearful fascination that he draws. "A great storm" at one time comes down upon him, "piece by piece," which "handled him twenty times worse than all he had met with before," while "floods of blasphemies were poured upon his spirit," and would "bolt out of his heart." He felt himself driven to commit the unpardonable sin and blaspheme the Holy Ghost, "whether he would or no." "No sin would serve but that." He was ready to "clap his hand under his chin," to keep his mouth shut, or to leap head-foremost "into some muckhill-hole," to prevent his uttering the fatal words.

At last he persuaded himself that he had committed the sin, and a good but not overwise man, "an ancient Christian," whom he consulted on his sad case, told him he thought so too, "which was but cold comfort." He thought himself possessed by the devil, and compared himself to a child "carried off under her apron by a gipsy." "Kick sometimes I did, and also shriek and cry, but yet I was as bound in the wings of the temptation, and the wind would carry me away." He wished himself "a dog or a toad," for they "had no soul to be lost as his was like to be;" and again a hopeless callousness seemed to settle upon him.

"If I would have given a thousand pounds for a tear I could not shed one; no, nor sometimes scarce desire to shed one." And yet he was all the while bewailing this hardness of heart, in which he thought himself singular. "This much sunk me. I thought my condition was alone; but how to get out of, or get rid of, these things I could not." Again the very ground of his faith was shaken. "Was the Bible true, or was it not rather a fable and cunning story?" All thought "their own religion true. Might not the Turks have as good Scriptures to prove their Mahomet Saviour as Christians had for Christ? What if all we believed in should be but 'a think-so' too?"

So powerful and so real were his illusions that he had hard work to keep himself from praying to things about him, to "a bush, a bull, a besom, or the like," or even to Satan himself. He heard voices behind him crying out that Satan desired to have him, and that "so loud and plain that he would turn his head to see who was calling him;" when on his knees in prayer he fancied he felt the foul fiend pull his clothes from behind, bidding him "break off, make haste; you have prayed enough."

This "horror of great darkness" was not always upon him. Bunyan had his intervals of "sunshine-weather" when Giant Despair's fits came on him, and the giant "lost the use of his hand." Texts of Scripture would give him a "sweet glance," and flood his soul with comfort. But these intervals of happiness were but short-lived. They were but "hints, touches, and short visits," sweet when present, but "like Peter's sheet, suddenly caught up again into heaven." But, though transient, they helped the burdened Pilgrim onward. So vivid was the impression sometimes made, that years after he could specify the place where these beams of sunlight fell on him—"sitting in a neighbour's house,"—"travelling into the country,"—as he was "going home from sermon." And the joy was real while it lasted. The words of the preacher's text, "Behold, thou art fair, my love," kindling his spirit, he felt his "heart filled with comfort and hope."

"Now I could believe that my sins would be forgiven." He was almost beside himself with ecstasy. "I was now so taken with the love and mercy of God that I thought I could have spoken of it even to the very crows that sat upon the ploughed lands before me, had they been capable to have understood me." "Surely," he cried with gladness, "I will not forget this forty years hence." "But, alas! within less than forty days I began to question all again." It was the Valley of the Shadow of Death which Bunyan, like his own Pilgrim, was travelling through. But, as in his allegory, "by and by the day broke," and "the Lord did more fully and graciously discover Himself unto him."

"One day," he writes, "as I was musing on the wickedness and blasphemy of my heart, that scripture came into my mind, 'He hath made peace by the Blood of His Cross.' By which I was made to see, both again and again and again that day, that God and my soul were friends by this blood: Yea, I saw the justice of God and my sinful soul could embrace and kiss each other. This was a good day to me. I hope I shall not forget it." At another time the "glory and joy" of a passage in the Hebrews (2:14, 15) were "so weighty" that "I was once or twice ready to swoon as I sat, not with grief and trouble, but with solid joy and peace." "But, oh! now how was my soul led on from truth to truth by God; now had I evidence of my salvation from heaven, with many golden seals thereon all banging in my sight, and I would long that the last day were come, or that I were fourscore years old, that I might die quickly that my soul might be at rest."

At this time he fell in with an old tattered copy of Luther's "Commentary on the Galatians," "so old that it was ready to fall piece from piece if I did but turn it over." As he read, to his amazement and thankfulness, he found his own spiritual experience described. "It was as if his book had been written out of my heart." It greatly comforted him to find that his condition was not, as he had thought, solitary, but that others had known the same inward struggles. "Of all the books that ever he had seen," he deemed it "most fit for a wounded conscience." This book was also the means of awakening an intense love for the Saviour. "Now I found, as I thought, that I loved Christ dearly. Oh, methought my soul cleaved unto Him, my affections cleaved unto Him; I felt love to Him as hot as fire."

And very quickly, as he tells us, his "love was tried to some purpose." He became the victim of an extraordinary temptation—"a freak of fancy," Mr. Froude terms it—"fancy resenting the minuteness with which he watched his own emotions." He had "found Christ" and felt Him "most precious to his soul." He was now tempted to give Him up, "to sell and part with this most blessed Christ, to exchange Him for the things of this life; for anything." Nor was this a mere passing, intermittent delusion. "It lay upon me for the space of a year, and did follow me so continually that I was not rid of it one day in a month, no, not sometimes one hour in many days together, except when I was asleep."

Wherever he was, whatever he was doing day and night, in bed, at table, at work, a voice kept sounding in his ears, bidding him "sell Christ" for this or that. He could neither "eat his food, stoop for a pin, chop a stick, or cast his eyes on anything" but the hateful words were heard, "not once only, but a hundred times over, as fast as a man could speak, 'sell Him, sell Him, sell Him,'" and, like his own Christian in the dark valley, he could not determine whether they were suggestions of the Wicked One, or came from his own heart. The agony was so intense, while, for hours together, he struggled with the temptation, that his whole body was convulsed by it. It was no metaphorical, but an actual, wrestling with a tangible enemy. He "pushed and thrust with his hands and elbows," and kept still answering, as fast as the destroyer said "sell Him," "No, I will not, I will not, I will not! not for thousands, thousands, thousands of worlds!" at least twenty times together.

But the fatal moment at last came, and the weakened will yielded, against itself. One morning as he lay in his bed, the voice came again with redoubled force, and would not be silenced. He fought against it as long as he could, "even until I was almost out of breath," when "without any conscious action of his will" the suicidal words shaped themselves in his heart, "Let Him go if He will."

Now all was over. He had spoken the words and they could not be recalled. Satan had "won the battle," and "as a bird that is shot from the top of a tree, down fell he into great guilt and fearful despair." He left his bed, dressed, and went "moping into the field," where for the next two hours he was "like a man bereft of life, and as one past all recovery and bound to eternal punishment." The most terrible examples in the Bible came trooping before him. He had sold his birthright like Esau. He a betrayed his Master like Judas—"I was ashamed that I should be like such an ugly man as Judas."

There was no longer any place for repentance. He was past all recovery; shut up unto the judgment to come. He dared hardly pray. When he tried to do so, he was "as with a tempest driven away from God," while something within said, "'Tis too late; I am lost; God hath let me fall." The texts which once had comforted him gave him no comfort now; or, if they did, it was but for a brief space. "About ten or eleven o'clock one day, as I was walking under a hedge and bemoaning myself for this hard hap that such a thought should arise within me, suddenly this sentence bolted upon me, 'The blood of Christ cleanseth from all sin,'" and gave me "good encouragement."

ut in two or three hours all was gone. The terrible words concerning Esau's selling his birthright took possession of his mind, and "held him down." This "stuck with him." Though he "sought it carefully with tears," there was no restoration for him. His agony received a terrible aggravation from a highly coloured narrative of the terrible death of Francis Spira, an Italian lawyer of the middle of the sixteenth century, who, having embraced the Protestant religion, was induced by worldly motives to return to the Roman Catholic Church, and died full of remorse and despair, from which Bunyan afterwards drew the awful picture of "the man in the Iron Cage" at "the Interpreter's house." The reading of this book was to his "troubled spirit" as "salt when rubbed into a fresh wound," "as knives and daggers in his soul."

We cannot wonder that his health began to give way under so protracted a struggle. His naturally sturdy frame was "shaken by a continual trembling." He would "wind and twine and shrink under his burden," the weight of which so crushed him that he "could neither stand, nor go, nor lie, either at rest or quiet." His digestion became disordered, and a pain, "as if his breastbone would have split asunder," made him fear that as he had been guilty of Judas' sin, so he was to perish by Judas' end, and "burst asunder in the midst."

In the trembling of his limbs he saw Cain's mark set upon him; God had marked him out for his curse. No one was ever so bad as he. No one had ever sinned so flagrantly. When he compared his sins with those of David and Solomon and Manasseh and others which had been pardoned, he found his sin so much exceeded theirs that he could have no hope of pardon. Theirs, "it was true, were great sins; sins of a bloody colour. But none of them were of the nature of his. He had sold his Saviour. His sin was point blank against Christ." "Oh, methought this sin was bigger than the sins of a country, of a kingdom, or of the whole world; not all of them together was able to equal mine; mine outwent them every one."

It would be wearisome to follow Bunyan through all the mazes of his self-torturing illusions. Fierce as the storm was, and long in its duration —for it was more than two years before the storm became a calm—the waves, though he knew it not, in their fierce tossings which threatened to drive his soul like a broken vessel headlong on the rocks of despair, were bearing him nearer and nearer to the "haven where he would be." His vivid imagination, as we have seen, surrounded him with audible voices. He had heard, as he thought, the tempter bidding him "Sell Christ;" now he thought he heard God "with a great voice, as it were, over his shoulder behind him," saying, "Return unto Me, for I have redeemed thee;" and though he felt that the voice mocked him, for he could not return, there was "no place of repentance" for him, and fled from it, it still pursued him, "holloaing after him, 'Return, return!'"

And return he did, but not all at once, or without many a fresh struggle. With his usual graphic power he describes the zigzag path by which he made his way. His hot and cold fits alternated with fearful suddenness. "As Esau beat him down, Christ raised him up." "His life hung in doubt, not knowing which way he should tip." More sensible evidence came. "One day," he tells us, "as I walked to and fro in a good man's shop"—we can hardly be wrong in placing it in Bedford—"bemoaning myself for this hard hap of mine, for that I should commit so great a sin, greatly fearing that I should not be pardoned, and ready to sink with fear, suddenly there was as if there had rushed in at the window the noise of wind upon me, but very pleasant, and I heard a voice speaking, 'Did'st ever refuse to be justified by the Blood of Christ?'"

Whether the voice were supernatural or not, he was not, "in twenty years' time," able to determine. At the time he thought it was. It was "as if an angel had come upon me." "It commanded a great calm upon me. It persuaded me there might be hope." But this persuasion soon vanished. "In three or four days I began to despair again." He found it harder than ever to pray. The devil urged that God was weary of him; had been weary for years past; that he wanted to get rid of him and his "bawlings in his ears," and therefore He had let him commit this particular sin that he might be cut off altogether. For such an one to pray was but to add sin to sin. There was no hope for him. Christ might indeed pity him and wish to help him; but He could not, for this sin was unpardonable. He had said "let Him go if He will," and He had taken him at his word.

"Then," he says, "I was always sinking whatever I did think or do." Years afterwards he remembered how, in this time of hopelessness, having walked one day, to a neighbouring town, wearied out with his misery, he sat down on a settle in the street to ponder over his fearful state. As he looked up, everything he saw seemed banded together for the destruction of so vile a sinner. The "sun grudged him its light, the very stones in the streets and the tiles on the house-roofs seemed to bend themselves against him." He burst forth with a grievous sigh, "How can God comfort such a wretch as I?" Comfort was nearer than he imagined. "No sooner had I said it, but this returned to me, as an echo doth answer a voice, 'This sin is not unto death.'"

This breathed fresh life into his soul. He was "as if he had been raised out of a grave." "It was a release to me from my former bonds, a shelter from my former storm." But though the storm was allayed it was by no means over. He had to struggle hard to maintain his ground. "Oh, how did Satan now lay about him for to bring me down again. But he could by no means do it, for this sentence stood like a millpost at my back."

But after two days the old despairing thoughts returned, "nor could his faith retain the word." A few hours, however, saw the return of his hopes. As he was on his knees before going to bed, "seeking the Lord with strong cries," a voice echoed his prayer, "I have loved Thee with an everlasting love." "Now I went to bed at quiet, and when I awaked the next morning it was fresh upon my soul and I believed it."

These voices from heaven—whether real or not he could not tell, nor did he much care, for they were real to him—were continually sounding in his ears to help him out of the fresh crises of his spiritual disorder. At one time "O man, great is thy faith," "fastened on his heart as if one had clapped him on the back." At another, "He is able," spoke suddenly and loudly within his heart; at another, that "piece of a sentence," "My grace is sufficient," darted in upon him "three times together," and he was "as though he had seen the Lord Jesus look down through the tiles upon him," and was sent mourning but rejoicing home.

But it was still with him like an April sky. At one time bright sunshine, at another lowering clouds. The terrible words about Esau "returned on him as before," and plunged him in darkness, and then again some good words, "as it seemed writ in great letters," brought back the light of day. But the sunshine began to last longer than before, and the clouds were less heavy. The "visage" of the threatening texts was changed; "they looked not on him so grimly as before;" "that about Esau's birthright began to wax weak and withdraw and vanish." "Now remained only the hinder part of the tempest. The thunder was gone; only a few drops fell on him now and then."

The long-expected deliverance was at hand. As he was walking in the fields, still with some fears in his heart, the sentence fell upon his soul, "Thy righteousness is in heaven." He looked up and "saw with the eyes of his soul our Saviour at God's right hand."

"There, I say, was my righteousness; so that wherever I was, or whatever I was a-doing, God could not say of me, 'He wants my righteousness,' for that was just before Him. Now did the chains fall off from my legs. I was loosed from my affliction and irons. My temptations also fled away, so that from that time those dreadful Scriptures left off to trouble me. Oh methought Christ, Christ, there was nothing but Christ that was before mine eyes. I could look from myself to Him, and should reckon that all those graces of God that now were green upon me, were yet but like those crack-groats, and fourpence-halfpennies that rich men carry in their purses, while their gold is in their trunks at home. Oh, I saw my gold was in my trunk at home."

"In Christ my Lord and Saviour. Further the Lord did lead me into the mystery of union with the Son of God. His righteousness was mine, His merits mine, His victory also mine. Now I could see myself in heaven and earth at once; in heaven by my Christ, by my Head, by my Righteousness and Life, though on earth by my body or person. These blessed considerations were made to spangle in mine eyes. Christ was my all; all my Wisdom, all my Righteousness, all my Sanctification, and all my Redemption."

Chapter 3

The Pilgrim, having now floundered through the Slough of Despond, passed through the Wicket Gate, climbed the Hill Difficulty, and got safe by the Lions, entered the Palace Beautiful, and was "had in to the family."

In plain words, Bunyan united himself to the little Christian brotherhood at Bedford, of which the former loose-living royalist major, Mr. Gifford, was the pastor, and was formally admitted into their society. In Gifford we recognize the prototype of the Evangelist of "The Pilgrim's Progress," while the Prudence, Piety, and Charity of Bunyan's immortal narrative had their human representatives in devout female members of the congregation, known in their little Bedford world as Sister Bosworth, Sister Munnes, and Sister Fenne, three of the poor women whose pleasant words on the things of God, as they sat at a doorway in the sun, "as if joy did make them speak," had first opened Bunyan's eyes to his spiritual ignorance. He was received into the church by baptism, which, according to his earliest biographer, Charles Doe "the Struggler," was performed publicly by Mr. Gifford, in the river Ouse, the "Bedford river" into which Bunyan tells us he once fell out of a boat, and barely escaped drowning. This was about the year 1653. The exact date is uncertain.

Bunyan never mentions his baptism himself, and the church books of Gifford's congregation do not commence till May, 1656, the year after Gifford's death. He was also admitted to the Holy Communion, which for want, as he deemed, of due reverence in his first approach to it, became the occasion of a temporary revival of his old temptations. While actually at the Lord's Table he was "forced to bend himself to pray" to be kept from uttering blasphemies against the ordinance itself, and cursing his fellow communicants. For three-quarters of a year he could "never have rest or ease" from this shocking perversity.

The constant strain of beating off this persistent temptation seriously affected his health. "Captain Consumption," who carried off his own "Mr. Badman," threatened his life. But his naturally robust constitution "routed his forces," and brought him through what at one time he anticipated would prove a fatal illness. Again and again, during his period of indisposition, the Tempter took advantage of his bodily weakness to ply him with his former despairing questionings as to his spiritual state. That seemed as bad as bad could be. "Live he must not; die he dare not." He was repeatedly near giving up all for lost.

But a few words of Scripture brought to his mind would revive his drooping spirits, with a natural reaction on his physical health, and he became "well both in body and mind at once." "My sickness did presently vanish, and I walked comfortably in my work for God again." At another time, after three or four days of deep dejection, some words from the Epistle to the Hebrews "came bolting in upon him," and sealed his sense of acceptance with an assurance he never afterwards entirely lost. "Then with joy I told my wife, 'Now I know, I know.' That night was a good night to me; I never had but few better. I could scarce lie in my bed for joy and peace and triumph through Christ."

During this time Bunyan, though a member of the Bedford congregation, continued to reside at Elstow, in the little thatched wayside tenement, with its lean-to forge at one end, already mentioned, which is still pointed out as "Bunyan's Cottage." There his two children, Mary, his passionately loved blind daughter, and Elizabeth were born; the one in 1650, and the other in 1654. It was probably in the next year, 1655, that he finally quitted his native village and took up his residence in Bedford, and became a deacon of the congregation. About this time also he must have lost the wife to whom he owed so much.

Bunyan does not mention the event, and our only knowledge of it is from the conversation of his second wife, Elizabeth, with Sir Matthew

Hale. He sustained also an even greater loss in the death of his friend and comrade, Mr. Gifford, who died in September, 1655. The latter was succeeded by a young man named John Burton, of very delicate health, who was taken by death from his congregation, by whom he was much beloved, in September, 1660, four months after the restoration of the Monarchy and the Church. Burton thoroughly appreciated Bunyan's gifts, and stood sponsor for him on the publication of his first printed work.

This was a momentous year for Bunyan, for in it Dr. Brown has shown, by a "comparison of dates," that we may probably place the beginning of Bunyan's ministerial life. Bunyan was now in his twenty-seventh year, in the prime of his manly vigour, with a vivid imagination, ready speech, minute textual knowledge of the Bible, and an experience of temptation and the wiles of the evil one, such as few Christians of double his years have ever reached. "His gifts could not long be hid." The beginnings of that which was to prove the great work of his life were slender enough. As Mr. Froude says, "he was modest, humble, shrinking."

The members of his congregation, recognizing that he had "the gift of utterance" asked him to speak "a word of exhortation" to them. The request scared him. The most truly gifted are usually the least conscious of their gifts. At first it did much "dash and abash his spirit." But after earnest entreaty he gave way, and made one or two trials of his gift in private meetings, "though with much weakness and infirmity." The result proved the correctness of his brethren's estimate. The young tinker showed himself no common preacher. His words came home with power to the souls of his hearers, who "protested solemnly, as in the sight of God, that they were both affected and comforted by them, and gave thanks to the Father of mercies for the grace bestowed on him."

After this, as the brethren went out on their itinerating rounds to the villages about, they began to ask Bunyan to accompany them, and though he "durst not make use of his gift in an open way," he would sometimes, "yet more privately still, speak a word of admonition, with which his hearers professed their souls edified." That he had a real Divine call to the ministry became increasingly evident, both to himself and to others. His engagements of this kind multiplied. An entry in the Church book records "that Brother Bunyan being taken off by the preaching of the gospel" from his duties as deacon, another member was appointed in his room. His appointment to the ministry was not long delayed.

After "some solemn prayer with fasting," he was "called forth and appointed a preacher of the word," not, however, so much for the Bedford congregation as for the neighbouring villages. He did not however, like some, neglect his business, or forget to "show piety at home." He still continued his craft as a tinker, and that with industry and success. "God," writes an early biographer, "had increased his stores so that he lived in great credit among his neighbours." He speedily became famous as a preacher. People "came in by hundreds to hear the word, and that from all parts, though upon sundry and divers accounts,"—"some," as Southey writes, "to marvel, and some perhaps to mock."

Curiosity to hear the once profane tinker preach was not one of the least prevalent motives. But his word proved a word of power to many. Those "who came to scoff remained to pray." "I had not preached long," he says, "before some began to be touched and to be greatly afflicted in their minds." His success humbled and amazed him, as it must every true man who compares the work with the worker. "At first," he says, "I could not believe that God should speak by me to the heart of any man, still counting myself unworthy; and though I did put it from me that they should be awakened by me, still they would confess it and affirm it before the saints of God. They would also bless God for me—unworthy wretch that I am—and count me God's instrument that showed to them the way of salvation." He preached wherever he found opportunity, in woods, in barns, on village greens, or even in churches.

But he liked best to preach "in the darkest places of the country, where people were the furthest off from profession," where he could give the fullest scope to "the awakening and converting power" he possessed. His success as a preacher might have tempted him to vanity. But the conviction that he was but an instrument in the hand of a higher power kept it down. He saw that if he had gifts and wanted grace he was but as a "tinkling cymbal." "What, thought I, shall I be proud because I am a sounding brass? Is it so much to be a fiddle?" This thought was, "as it were, a maul on the head of the pride and vainglory" which he found "easily blown up at the applause and commendation of every unadvised christian." His experiences, like those of every public speaker, especially the most eloquent, were very varied, even in the course of the same sermon.

Sometimes, he tells us, he would begin "with much clearness, evidence, and liberty of speech," but, before he had done, he found himself "so straitened in his speech before the people," that he "scarce knew or remembered what he had been about," and felt "as if his head had been in a bag all the time of the exercise." He feared that he would not be able to "speak sense to the hearers," or he would be "seized with such faintness and strengthlessness that his legs were hardly able to carry him to his place of preaching."

Old temptations too came back. Blasphemous thoughts formed themselves into words, which he had hard work to keep himself from uttering from the pulpit. Or the tempter tried to silence him by telling him that what he was going to say would condemn himself, and he would go "full of guilt and terror even to the pulpit door." "'What,' the devil would say, 'will you preach this? Of this your own soul is guilty. Preach not of it at all, or if you do, yet so mince it as to make way for your own escape.'"

All, however, was in vain. Necessity was laid upon him. "Woe," he cried, "is me, if I preach not the gospel." His heart was "so wrapped up in the glory of this excellent work, that he counted himself more blessed and honoured of God than if he had made him emperor of the Christian world."

Bunyan was no preacher of vague generalities. He knew that sermons miss their mark if they hit no one. Self-application is their object.

"Wherefore," he says, "I laboured so to speak the word, as that the sin and person guilty might be particularized by it." And what he preached he knew and felt to be true. It was not what he read in books, but what he had himself experienced. Like Dante he had been in hell himself, and could speak as one who knew its terrors, and could tell also of the blessedness of deliverance by the person and work of Christ.

And this consciousness gave him confidence and courage in declaring his message. It was "as if an angel of God had stood at my back." "Oh it hath been with such power and heavenly evidence upon my own soul while I have been labouring to fasten it upon the conscience of others, that I could not be contented with saying, 'I believe and am sure.' Methought I was more than sure, if it be lawful so to express myself, that the things I asserted were true."

Bunyan, like all earnest workers for God, had his disappointments which wrung his heart. He could be satisfied with nothing less than the conversion and sanctification of his hearers. "If I were fruitless, it mattered not who commanded me; but if I were fruitful, I cared not who did condemn." And the result of a sermon was often very different from what he anticipated: "When I thought I had done no good, then I did the most; and when I thought I should catch them, I fished for nothing." "A word cast in by-the-bye sometimes did more execution than all the Sermon besides." The tie between him and his spiritual children was very close. The backsliding of any of his converts caused him the most extreme grief; "it was more to me than if one of my own children were going to the grave. Nothing hath gone so near me as that, unless it was the fear of the loss of the salvation of my own soul."

A story, often repeated, but too characteristic to be omitted, illustrates the power of his preaching even in the early days of his ministry. "Being to preach in a church in a country village in Cambridgeshire"—it was before the Restoration—"and the public being gathered together in the churchyard, a Cambridge scholar, and none of the soberest neither, inquired what the meaning of that concourse of people was (it being a week-day); and being told that one Bunyan, a tinker, was to preach there, he gave a lad twopence to hold his horse, saying he was resolved to hear the tinker prate; and so he went into the church to hear him.

But God met him there by His ministry, so that he came out much changed; and would by his good will hear none but the tinker for a long time after, he himself becoming a very eminent preacher in that country afterwards." "This story," continues the anonymous biographer, "I know to be true, having many times discoursed with the man." To the same ante-Restoration period, Dr. Brown also assigns the anecdote of Bunyan's encounter, on the road near Cambridge, with the university man who asked him how he dared to preach not having the original Scriptures.

With ready wit, Bunyan turned the tables on the scholar by asking whether he had the actual originals, the copies written by the apostles and prophets. The scholar replied, "No," but they had what they believed to be a true copy of the original. "And I," said Bunyan, "believe the English Bible to be a true copy, too." "Then away rid the scholar."

The fame of such a preacher, naturally, soon spread far and wide; all the countryside flocked eagerly to hear him. In some places, as at Meldreth in Cambridgeshire, and Yelden in his own county of Bedfordshire, the pulpits of the parish churches were opened to him. At Yelden, the Rector, Dr. William Dell, the Puritan Master of Caius College, Cambridge, formerly Chaplain to the army under Fairfax, roused the indignation of his orthodox parishioners by allowing him—"one Bunyon of Bedford, a tinker," as he is ignominiously styled in the petition sent up to the House of Lords in 1660—to preach in his parish church on Christmas Day. But, generally, the parochial clergy were his bitterest enemies.

"When I first went to preach the word abroad," he writes, "the Doctors and priests of the country did open wide against me." Many were envious of his success where they had so signally failed. In the words of Mr. Henry Deane, when defending Bunyan against the attacks of Dr. T. Smith, Professor of Arabic and Keeper of the University Library at

Cambridge, who had come upon Bunyan preaching in a barn at Toft, they were "angry with the tinker because he strove to mend souls as well as kettles and pans," and proved himself more skilful in his craft than those who had graduated at a university.

Envy is ever the mother of detraction. Slanders of the blackest dye against his moral character were freely circulated, and as readily believed. It was the common talk that he was a thorough reprobate. Nothing was too bad for him. He was "a witch, a Jesuit, a highwayman, and the like." It was reported that he had "his misses and his bastards; that he had two wives at once," &c. Such charges roused all the man in Bunyan. Few passages in his writings show more passion than that in "Grace Abounding," in which he defends himself from the "fools or knaves" who were their authors. He "begs belief of no man, and if they believe him or disbelieve him it is all one to him.

But he would have them know how utterly baseless their accusations are." "My foes," he writes, "have missed their mark in their open shooting at me. I am not the man. If all the fornicators and adulterers in England were hanged by the neck till they be dead, John Bunyan would be still alive. I know not whether there is such a thing as a woman breathing under the copes of the whole heaven but by their apparel, their children, or by common fame, except my wife." He calls not only men, but angels, nay, even God Himself, to bear testimony to his innocence in this respect. But though they were so absolutely baseless, nay, the rather because they were so baseless, the grossness of these charges evidently stung Bunyan very deeply.

So bitter was the feeling aroused against him by the marvellous success of his irregular ministry, that his enemies, even before the restoration of the Church and Crown, endeavoured to put the arm of the law in motion to restrain him. We learn from the church books that in March, 1658, the little Bedford church was in trouble for "Brother Bunyan," against whom an indictment had been laid at the Assizes for "preaching at Eaton Socon." Of this indictment we hear no more; so it was probably dropped. But it is an instructive fact that, even during the boasted religious liberty of the Protectorate, irregular preaching, especially that of the much dreaded Anabaptists, was an indictable offence.

But, as Dr. Brown observes, "religious liberty had not yet come to mean liberty all round, but only liberty for a certain recognized section of Christians." That there was no lack of persecution during the Commonwealth is clear from the cruel treatment to which Quakers were subjected, to say nothing of the intolerance shown to Episcopalians and Roman Catholics. In Bunyan's own county of Bedford, Quakeresses were sentenced to be whipped and sent to Bridewell for reproving a parish priest, perhaps well deserving of it, and exhorting the folks on a market day to repentance and amendment of life.

"The simple truth is," writes Robert Southey, "all parties were agreed on the one eatholic opinion that certain doctrines were not to be tolerated:" the only points of difference between them were "what those doctrines were," and how far intolerance might be carried. The withering lines are familiar to us, in which Milton denounces the "New Forcers of Conscience," who by their intolerance and "supermetropolitan and hyperarchiepiscopal tyranny," proved that in his proverbial words, "New Presbyter is but old Priest writ large"—

> Because you have thrown off your prelate lord,
> And with stiff vows renounce his liturgy
> Dare ye for this adjure the civil sword
> To force our consciences that Christ set free!

How Bunyan came to escape we know not. But the danger he was in was imminent enough for the church at Bedford to meet to pray "for counsail what to doe" in respect of it.

It was in these closing years of the Protectorate that Bunyan made his first essay at authorship. He was led to it by a long and tiresome controversy with the Quakers, who had recently found their way to Bedford. The foundations of the faith, he thought, were being undermined. The Quakers' teaching as to the inward light seemed to him a serious disparagement of the Holy Scriptures, while their mystical view of the spiritual Christ revealed to the soul and dwelling in the heart, came perilously near to a denial of the historic reality of the personal Christ. He had had public disputations with male and female Quakers from time to time, at the Market Cross at Bedford, at "Paul's Steeple-house in Bedford town," and other places. One of them, Anne Blackley by name, openly bade him throw away the Scriptures, to which Bunyan replied, "No; for then the devil would be too hard for me." The same enthusiast charged him with "preaching up an idol, and using conjuration and witchcraft," because of his assertion of the bodily presence of Christ in heaven.

The first work of one who was to prove himself so voluminous an author, cannot but be viewed with much interest. It was a little volume in duodecimo, of about two hundred pages, entitled "Some Gospel Truths Opened, by that unworthy servant of Christ, John Bunyan, of Bedford, by the Grace of God, preacher of the Gospel of His dear Son," published in 1656. The little book, which, as Dr. Brown says, was "evidently thrown off at a heat," was printed in London and published at Newport Pagnel. Bunyan being entirely unknown to the world, his first literary venture was introduced by a commendatory "Epistle" written by Gifford's successor, John Burton.

In this Burton speaks of the young author—Bunyan was only in his twenty-ninth year—as one who had "neither the greatness nor the wisdom of the world to commend him," "not being chosen out of an earthly but out of a heavenly university, the Church of Christ," where "through grace he had taken three heavenly degrees, to wit, union with Christ, the anointing of the Spirit, and experience of the temptations of Satan," and as one of whose "soundness in the faith, godly conversation, and his ability to preach the Gospel, not by human aid, but by the Spirit of the Lord," he "with many other saints had had experience."

This book must be pronounced a very remarkable production for a young travelling tinker, under thirty, and without any literary or theological training but such as he had gained for himself after attaining to manhood. Its arrangement is excellent, the arguments are ably marshalled, the style is clear, the language pure and well chosen. It is, in the main, a well-reasoned defence of the historical truth of the Articles of the Creed relating to the Second Person of the Trinity, against the mystical teaching of the followers of George Fox, who, by a false spiritualism, sublimated the whole Gospel narrative into a vehicle for the representation of truths relating to the inner life of the believer.

No one ever had a firmer grasp than Bunyan of the spiritual bearing of the facts of the recorded life of Christ on the souls of men. But he would not suffer their "subjectivity"—to adopt modern terms—to destroy their "objectivity." If the Son of God was not actually born of the Virgin Mary, if He did not live in a real human body, and in that body die, lie in the grave, rise again, and ascend up into heaven, whence He would return—and that Bunyan believed shortly—in the same Body He took of His mortal mother, His preaching was vain; their faith was vain; they were yet in their sins. Those who "cried up a Christ within, in opposition to a Christ without," who asserted that Christ had no other Body but the Church, that the only Crucifixion, rising again, and ascension of Christ was that within the believer, and that every man had, as an inner light, a measure of Christ's Spirit within him sufficient to guide him to salvation, he asserted were "possessed with a spirit of delusion;" deceived themselves, they were deceiving others to their eternal ruin.

To the refutation of such fundamental errors, substituting a mystical for an historical faith, Bunyan's little treatise is addressed; and it may be truly said the work is done effectually. To adopt Coleridge's expression concerning Bunyan's greater and world-famous work, it is an admirable "Summa Theologiæ Evangelicæ," which, notwithstanding its obsolete style and old-fashioned arrangement, may be read even now with advantage.

Bunyan's denunciation of the tenets of the Quakers speedily elicited a reply. This was written by a certain Edward Burrough, a young man of three and twenty, fearless, devoted, and ardent in the propagation of the tenets of his sect. Being subsequently thrown into Newgate with hundreds of his co-religionists, at the same time that his former antagonist was imprisoned in Bedford Gaol, Burrough met the fate Bunyan's stronger constitution enabled him to escape; and in the language of the times, "rotted in prison," a victim to the loathsome foulness of his place of incarceration, in the year of the "Bartholomew Act," 1662.

Burrough entitled his reply, "The Gospel of Peace, contended for in the Spirit of Meekness and Love against the secret opposition of John Bunyan, a professed minister in Bedfordshire." His opening words, too characteristic of the entire treatise, display but little of the meekness professed. "How long, ye crafty fowlers, will ye prey upon the innocent? How long shall the righteous be a prey to your teeth, ye subtle foxes! Your dens are in darkness, and your mischief is hatched upon your beds of secret whoredoms?"

Of John Burton and the others who recommended Bunyan's treatise, he says, "They have joined themselves with the broken army of Magog, and have showed themselves in the defence of the dragon against the Lamb in the day of war betwixt them." We may well echo Dr. Brown's wish that "these two good men could have had a little free and friendly talk face to face. There would probably have been better understanding, and fewer hard words, for they were really not so far apart as they thought. Bunyan believed in the inward light, and Burrough surely accepted an objective Christ. But failing to see each other's exact point of view, Burrough thunders at Bunyan, and Bunyan swiftly returns the shot."

The rapidity of Bunyan's literary work is amazing, especially when we take his antecedents into account. Within a few weeks he published his rejoinder to Friend Burrough, under the title of "A Vindication of Gospel Truths Opened." In this work, which appeared in 1667, Bunyan repays Burrough in his own coin, styling him "a proved enemy to the truth," a "grossly railing Rabshakeh, who breaks out with a taunt and a jeer," is very "censorious and utters many words without knowledge." In vigorous, nervous language, which does not spare his opponent, he defends himself from Burrough's charges, and proves that the Quakers are "deceivers."

"As for you thinking that to drink water, and wear no hatbands is not walking after your own lusts, I say that whatsoever man do make a religion out of, having no warrant for it in Scripture, is but walking after their own lusts, and not after the Spirit of God." Burrough had most unwarrantably stigmatized Bunyan as one of "the false prophets, who love the wages of unrighteousness, and through covetousness make merchandise of souls." Bunyan calmly replies, "Friend, dost thou speak this as from thy own knowledge, or did any other tell thee so? However that spirit that led thee out this way is a lying spirit. For though I be poor and of no repute in the world as to outward things, yet through grace I have learned by the example of the Apostle to preach the truth, and also to work with my hands both for mine own living, and for those that are with me, when I have opportunity. And I trust that the Lord Jesus who hath helped me to reject the wages of unrighteousness hitherto, will also help me still so that I shall distribute that which God hath given me freely, and not for filthy lucre's sake."

The fruitfulness of his ministry which Burrough had called in question, charging him with having "run before he was sent," he refuses to discuss. Bunyan says, "I shall leave it to be taken notice of by the people of God and the country where I dwell, who will testify the contrary for me, setting aside the carnal ministry with their retinue who are so mad against me as thyself."

In his third book, published in 1658, at "the King's Head, in the Old Bailey," a few days before Oliver Cromwell's death, Bunyan left the thorny domain of polemics, for that of Christian exhortation, in which his chief work was to be done. This work was an exposition of the parable of "the Rich Man and Lazarus," bearing the horror-striking title, "A Few Sighs from Hell, or the Groans of a Damned Soul." In this work, as its title would suggest, Bunyan, accepting the literal accuracy of the parable as a description of the realities of the world beyond the grave, gives full scope to his vivid imagination in portraying the condition of the lost. It contains some touches of racy humour, especially in the similes, and is written in the nervous homespun English of which he was master.

Its popularity is shown by its having gone through nine editions in the author's lifetime. To take an example or two of its style: dealing with the excuses people make for not hearing the Gospel, "O, saith one, I dare not for my master, my brother, my landlord; I shall lose his favour, his house of work, and so decay my calling. O, saith another, I would willingly go in this way but for my father; he chides me and tells me he will not stand my friend when I come to want; I shall never enjoy a pennyworth of his goods; he will disinherit me—And I dare not, saith another, for my husband, for he will be a-railing, and tells me he will turn me out of doors, he will beat me and cut off my legs;" and then turning from the hindered to the hinderers: "Oh, what red lines will there be against all those rich ungodly landlords that so keep under their poor tenants that they dare not go out to hear the word for fear that their rent should be raised or they turned out of their houses. Think on this, you drunken proud rich, and scornful landlords; think on this, you madbrained blasphemous husbands, that are against the godly and chaste conversation of your wives; also you that hold your servants so hard to it that you will not spare them time to hear the Word, unless it will be where and when your lusts will let you."

He bids the ungodly consider that "the profits, pleasures, and vanities of the world" will one day "give thee the slip, and leave thee in the sands and the brambles of all that thou hast done." The careless man lies "like the smith's dog at the foot of the anvil, though the fire sparks flee in his face." The rich man remembers how he once despised Lazarus, "scrubbed beggarly Lazarus. What, shall I dishonour my fair sumptuous and gay house with such a scabbed creephedge as he? The Lazaruses are not allowed to warn them of the wrath to come, because they are not gentlemen, because they cannot with Pontius Pilate speak Hebrew, Greek, and Latin. Nay, they must not, shall not, speak to them, and all because of this."

The fourth production of Bunyan's pen, his last book before his twelve years of prison life began, is entitled, "The Doctrine of Law and Grace Unfolded." With a somewhat overstrained humility which is hardly worthy of him, he describes himself in the title-page as "that poor contemptible creature John Bunyan, of Bedford." It was given to the world in May, 1659, and issued from the same press in the Old Bailey as his last work. It cannot be said that this is one of Bunyan's most attractive writings. It is as he describes it, "a parcel of plain yet sound, true, and home sayings," in which with that clearness of thought and accuracy of arrangement which belongs to him, and that marvellous acquaintance with Scripture language which he had gained by his constant study of the Bible, he sets forth the two covenants—the covenant of works, and the covenant of Grace—"in their natures, ends, bounds, together with the state and condition of them that are under the one, and of them that are under the other."

Dr. Brown describes the book as "marked by a firm grasp of faith and a strong view of the reality of Christ's person and work as the one Priest and Mediator for a sinful world." To quote a passage, "Is there righteousness in Christ? that is mine. Is there perfection in that righteousness? that is mine. Did He bleed for sin? It was for mine. Hath He overcome the law, the devil, and hell? The victory is mine, and I am come forth conqueror, nay, more than a conqueror through Him that hath loved me... Lord, show me continually in the light of Thy Spirit, through Thy word, that Jesus that was born in the days of Cæsar Augustus, when Mary, a daughter of Judah, went with Joseph to be taxed in Bethlehem, that He is the very Christ. Let me not rest contented without such a faith that is so wrought even by the discovery of His Birth, Crucifying Death, Blood, Resurrection, Ascension, and Second—which is His Personal—Coming again, that the very faith of it may fill my soul with comfort and holiness."

Up and down its pages we meet with vivid reminiscences of his own career, of which he can only speak with wonder and thankfulness. In the "Epistle to the Reader," which introduces it, occurs the passage already referred to describing his education. "I never went to school to Aristotle or Plato, but was brought up at my father's house in a very mean condition, among a company of poor countrymen." Of his own religious state before his conversion he thus speaks: "When it pleased the Lord to begin to instruct my soul, He found me one of the black sinners of the world. He found me making a sport of oaths, and also of lies; and many a soul-poisoning meal did I make out of divers lusts, such as drinking, dancing, playing, pleasure with the wicked ones of the world; and so wedded was I to my sins, that thought I to myself, 'I will have them though I lose my soul.'" And then, after narrating the struggles he had had with his conscience, the alternations of hope and fear which he passed through, which are more fully described in his "Grace Abounding," he thus vividly depicts the full assurance of faith he had attained to: "I saw through grace that it was the Blood shed on Mount Calvary that did save and redeem sinners, as clearly and as really with the eyes of my soul as ever, methought, I had seen a penny loaf bought with a penny… O let the saints know that unless the devil can pluck Christ out of heaven he cannot pull a true believer out of Christ."

In a striking passage he shows how, by turning Satan's temptations against himself, Christians may "Get the art as to outrun him in his own shoes, and make his own darts pierce himself." "What! didst thou never learn to outshoot the devil in his own bow, and cut off his head with his own sword as David served Goliath?" The whole treatise is somewhat wearisome, but the pious reader will find much in it for spiritual edification.

Chapter 4

We cannot doubt that one in whom loyalty was so deep and fixed a principle as Bunyan, would welcome with sincere thankfulness the termination of the miserable interval of anarchy which followed the death of the Protector and the abdication of his indolent and feeble son, by the restoration of monarchy in the person of Charles the Second. Even if some forebodings might have arisen that with the restoration of the old monarchy the old persecuting laws might be revived, which made it criminal for a man to think for himself in the matters which most nearly concerned his eternal interests, and to worship in the way which he found most helpful to his spiritual life, they would have been silenced by the promise, contained in Charles's "Declaration from Breda," of liberty to tender consciences, and the assurance that no one should be disquieted for differences of opinion in religion, so long as such differences did not endanger the peace and well-being of the realm. If this declaration meant anything, it meant a breadth of toleration larger and more liberal than had been ever granted by Cromwell. Any fears of the renewal of persecution must be groundless.

But if such dreams of religious liberty were entertained they were speedily and rudely dispelled, and Bunyan was one of the first to feel the shock of the awakening. The promise was coupled with a reference to the "mature deliberation of Parliament." With such a promise Charles's easy conscience was relieved of all responsibility. Whatever he might promise, the nation, and Parliament which was its mouthpiece, might set his promise aside. And if he knew anything of the temper of the people he was returning to govern, he must have felt assured that any scheme of comprehension was certain to be rejected by them.

As Mr. Froude has said, "before toleration is possible, men must have learnt to tolerate toleration," and this was a lesson the English nation was very far from having learnt; at no time, perhaps, were they further from it. Puritanism had had its day, and had made itself generally detested. Deeply enshrined as it was in many earnest and devout hearts, such as Bunyan's, it was necessarily the religion not of the many, but of the few; it was the religion not of the common herd, but of a spiritual aristocracy. Its stern condemnation of all mirth and pastime, as things in their nature sinful, of which we have so many evidences in Bunyan's own writings; its repression of all that makes life brighter and more joyous, and the sour sanctimoniousness which frowned upon innocent relaxation, had rendered its yoke unbearable to ordinary human nature, and men took the earliest opportunity of throwing the yoke off and trampling it under foot. They hailed with rude and boisterous rejoicings the restoration of the Monarchy which they felt, with a true instinct, involved the restoration of the old Church of England, the church of their fathers and of the older among themselves, with its larger indulgence for the instincts of humanity, its wider comprehensiveness, and its more dignified and decorous ritual.

The reaction from Puritanism pervaded all ranks. In no class, however, was its influence more powerful than among the country gentry. Most of them had been severe sufferers both in purse and person during the Protectorate. Fines and sequestrations had fallen heavily upon them, and they were eager to retaliate on their oppressors. Their turn had come; can we wonder that they were eager to use it?

As Mr. J. R. Green has said: "The Puritan, the Presbyterian, the Commonwealthsman, all were at their feet. . . Their whole policy appeared to be dictated by a passionate spirit of reaction. . . The oppressors of the parson had been the oppressors of the squire. The sequestrator who had driven the one from his parsonage had driven the other from his manor-house. Both had been branded with the same charge of malignity. Both had suffered together, and the new Parliament was resolved that both should triumph together."

The feeling thus eloquently expressed goes far to explain the harshness which Bunyan experienced at the hands of the administrators of justice at the crisis of his life at which we have now arrived. Those before whom he was successively arraigned belonged to this very class, which, having suffered most severely during the Puritan usurpation, was least likely to show consideration to a leading teacher of the Puritan body. Nor were reasons wanting to justify their severity. The circumstances of the times were critical.

The public mind was still in an excitable state, agitated by the wild schemes of political and religious enthusiasts plotting to destroy the whole existing framework both of Church and State, and set up their own chimerical fabric. We cannot be surprised that, as Southey has said, after all the nation had suffered from fanatical zeal, "The government, rendered suspicious by the constant sense of danger, was led as much by fear as by resentment to seventies which are explained by the necessities of self-defence," and which the nervous apprehensions of the nation not only condoned, but incited.

Already Churchmen in Wales had been taking the law into their own hands, and manifesting their orthodoxy by harrying Quakers and Nonconformists. In the May and June of this year, we hear of sectaries being taken from their beds and haled to prison, and brought manacled to the Quarter Sessions and committed to loathsome dungeons. Matters had advanced since then. The Church had returned in its full power and privileges together with the monarchy, and everything went back into its old groove.

Every Act passed for the disestablishment and disendowment of the Church was declared a dead letter. Those of the ejected incumbents who remained alive entered again into their parsonages, and occupied their pulpits as of old; the surviving bishops returned to their sees; and the whole existing statute law regarding the Church revived from its suspended animation. No new enactment was required to punish Nonconformists and to silence their ministers; though, to the disgrace of the nation and its parliament, many new ones were subsequently passed, with ever-increasing disabilities.

The various Acts of Elizabeth supplied all that was needed. Under these Acts all who refused to attend public worship in their parish churches were subject to fines; while those who resorted to conventicles were to be imprisoned till they made their submissions; if at the end of three months they refused to submit they were to be banished the realm, and if they returned from banishment, without permission of the Crown, they were liable to execution as felons. This long-disused sword was now drawn from its rusty sheath to strike terror into the hearts of Nonconformists. It did not prove very effectual. All the true-hearted men preferred to suffer rather than yield in so sacred a cause. Bunyan was one of the earliest of these, as he proved one of the staunchest.

Early in October, 1660, the country magistrates meeting in Bedford issued an order for the public reading of the Liturgy of the Church of England. Such an order Bunyan would not regard as concerning him. Anyhow he would not give obeying it a thought. One of the things we least like in Bunyan is the feeling he exhibits towards the Book of Common Prayer. To him it was an accursed thing, the badge and token of a persecuting party, a relic of popery which he exhorted his adherents to "take heed that they touched not" if they would be "steadfast in the faith of Jesus Christ." Nothing could be further from his thoughts than to give any heed to the magistrates' order to go to church and pray "after the form of men's inventions."

The time for testing Bunyan's resolution was now near at hand. Within six months of the king's landing, within little more than a month of the issue of the magistrate's order for the use of the Common Prayer Book, his sturdy determination to yield obedience to no authority in spiritual matters but that of his own conscience was put to the proof. Bunyan may safely be regarded as at that time the most conspicuous of the Nonconformists of the neighbourhood. He had now preached for five or six years with ever-growing popularity. No name was so rife in men's mouths as his. At him, therefore, as the representative of his brother sectaries, the first blow was levelled. It is no cause of surprise that in the measures taken against him he recognized the direct agency of Satan to stop the course of the truth: "That old enemy of man's salvation," he says, "took his opportunity to inflame the hearts of his vassals against me, insomuch that at the last I was laid out for the warrant of a justice."

The circumstances were these, on November 12, 1660, Bunyan had engaged to go to the little hamlet of Lower Samsell near Harlington, to hold a religious service. His purpose becoming known, a neighbouring magistrate, Mr. Francis Wingate, of Harlington House, was instructed to issue a warrant for his apprehension under the Act of Elizabeth. The meeting being represented to him as one of seditious persons bringing arms, with a view to the disturbance of the public peace, he ordered that a strong watch should be kept about the house, "as if," Bunyan says, "we did intend to do some fearful business to the destruction of the country."

The intention to arrest him oozed out, and on Bunyan's arrival the whisperings of his friends warned him of his danger. He might have easily escaped if he "had been minded to play the coward." Some advised it, especially the brother at whose house the meeting was to take place. He, "living by them," knew "what spirit" the magistrates "were of," before whom Bunyan would be taken if arrested, and the small hope there would be of his avoiding being committed to gaol. The man himself, as a "harbourer of a conventicle," would also run no small danger of the same fate, but Bunyan generously acquits him of any selfish object in his warning: "he was, I think, more afraid of (for) me, than of (for) himself."

The matter was clear enough to Bunyan. At the same time it was not to be decided in a hurry. The time fixed for the service not being yet come, Bunyan went into the meadow by the house, and pacing up and down thought the question well out. "If he who had up to this time showed himself hearty and courageous in his preaching, and had made it his business to encourage others, were now to run and make an escape, it would be of an ill savour in the country.

If he were now to flee because there was a warrant out for him, would not the weak and newly-converted brethren be afraid to stand when great words only were spoken to them. God had, in His mercy, chosen him to go on the forlorn hope; to be the first to be opposed for the gospel; what a discouragement it must be to the whole body if he were to fly. No, he would never by any cowardliness of his give occasion to the enemy to blaspheme the gospel."

So back to the house he came with his mind made up. He had come to hold the meeting, and hold the meeting he would. He was not conscious of saying or doing any evil. If he had to suffer it was the Lord's will, and he was prepared for it. He had a full hour before him to escape if he had been so minded, but he was resolved "not to go away." He calmly waited for the time fixed for the brethren to assemble, and then, without hurry or any show of alarm, he opened the meeting in the usual manner, with prayer for God's blessing. He had given out his text, the brethren had just opened their Bibles and Bunyan was beginning to preach, when the arrival of the constable with the warrant put an end to the exercise.

Bunyan requested to be allowed to say a few parting words of encouragement to the terrified flock. This was granted, and he comforted the little company with the reflection that it was a mercy to suffer in so good a cause; and that it was better to be the persecuted than the persecutors; better to suffer as Christians than as thieves or murderers. The constable and the justice's servant soon growing weary of listening to Bunyan's exhortations, interrupted him and "would not be quiet till they had him away" from the house.

The justice who had issued the warrant, Mr. Wingate, not being at home that day, a friend of Bunyan's residing on the spot offered to house him for the night, undertaking that he should be forthcoming the next day. The following morning this friend took him to the constable's house, and they then proceeded together to Mr. Wingate's. A few inquiries showed the magistrate that he had entirely mistaken the character of the Samsell meeting and its object. Instead of a gathering of "Fifth Monarchy men," or other turbulent fanatics as he had supposed, for the disturbance of the public peace, he learnt from the constable that they were only a few peaceable, harmless people, met together "to preach and hear the word," without any political meaning.

Wingate was now at a nonplus, and "could not well tell what to say." For the credit of his magisterial character, however, he must do something to show that he had not made a mistake in issuing the warrant. So he asked Bunyan what business he had there, and why it was not enough for him to follow his own calling instead of breaking the law by preaching. Bunyan replied that his only object in coming there was to exhort his hearers for their souls' sake to forsake their sinful courses and close in with Christ, and this he could do and follow his calling as well. Wingate, now feeling himself in the wrong, lost his temper, and declared angrily that he would "break the neck of these unlawful meetings," and that Bunyan must find securities for his good behaviour or go to gaol. There was no difficulty in obtaining the security.

Bail was at once forthcoming. The real difficulty lay with Bunyan himself. No bond was strong enough to keep him from preaching. If his friends gave them, their bonds would be forfeited, for he "would not leave speaking the word of God." Wingate told him that this being so, he must be sent to gaol to be tried at the next Quarter Sessions, and left the room to make out his mittimus. While the committal was preparing, one whom Bunyan bitterly styles "an old enemy to the truth," Dr. Lindall, Vicar of Harlington, Wingate's father-in-law, came in and began "taunting at him with many reviling terms," demanding what right he had to preach and meddle with that for which he had no warrant, charging him with making long prayers to devour widows houses, and likening him to "one Alexander the Coppersmith he had read of," "aiming, 'tis like," says Bunyan, "at me because I was a tinker."

The mittimus was now made out, and Bunyan in the constable's charge was on his way to Bedford, when he was met by two of his friends, who begged the constable to wait a little while that they might use their interest with the magistrate to get Bunyan released. After a somewhat lengthened interview with Wingate, they returned with the message that if Bunyan would wait on the magistrate and "say certain words" to him, he might go free. To satisfy his friends, Bunyan returned with them, though not with any expectation that the engagement proposed to him would be such as he could lawfully take. "If the words were such as he could say with a good conscience he would say them, or else he would not."

After all this coming and going, by the time Bunyan and his friends got back to Harlington House, night had come on. As he entered the hall, one, he tells us, came out of an inner room with a lighted candle in his hand, whom Bunyan recognized as one William Foster, a lawyer of Bedford, Wingate's brother-in-law, afterwards a fierce persecutor of the Nonconformists of the district. With a simulated affection, "as if he would have leapt on my neck and kissed me," which put Bunyan on his guard, as he had ever known him for "a close opposer of the ways of God," he adopted the tone of one who had Bunyan's interest at heart, and begged him as a friend to yield a little from his stubbornness. His brother-in-law, he said, was very loath to send him to gaol.

All he had to do was only to promise that he would not call people together, and he should be set at liberty and might go back to his home. Such meetings were plainly unlawful and must be stopped. Bunyan had better follow his calling and leave off preaching, especially on week-days, which made other people neglect their calling too. God commanded men to work six days and serve Him on the seventh. It was vain for Bunyan to reply that he never summoned people to hear him, but that if they came he could not but use the best of his skill and wisdom to counsel them for their soul's salvation; that he could preach and the people could come to hear without neglecting their callings, and that men were bound to look out for their souls' welfare on week-days as well as Sundays.

Neither could convince the other. Bunyan's stubbornness was not a little provoking to Foster, and was equally disappointing to Wingate. They both evidently wished to dismiss the case, and intentionally provided a loophole for Bunyan's escape. The promise put into his mouth—"that he would not call the people together"—was purposely devised to meet his scrupulous conscience. But even if he could keep the promise in the letter, Bunyan knew that he was fully purposed to violate its spirit. He was the last man to forfeit self-respect by playing fast and loose with his conscience. All evasion was foreign to his nature. The long interview came to an end at last.

Once again Wingate and Foster endeavoured to break down Bunyan's resolution; but when they saw he was "at a point, and would not be moved or persuaded," the mittimus was again put into the constable's hands, and he and his prisoner were started on the walk to Bedford gaol. It was dark, as we have seen, when this protracted interview began. It must have now been deep in the night. Bunyan gives no hint whether the walk was taken in the dark or in the daylight. There was however no need for haste. Bedford was thirteen miles away, and the constable would probably wait till the morning to set out for the prison which was to be Bunyan's home for twelve long years, to which he went carrying, he says, the "peace of God along with me, and His comfort in my poor soul."

Chapter 5

A long-standing tradition has identified Bunyan's place of imprisonment with a little corporation lock-up-house, some fourteen feet square, picturesquely perched on one of the mid-piers of the many-arched mediæval bridge which, previously to 1765, spanned the Ouse at Bedford, and as Mr. Froude has said, has "furnished a subject for pictures," both of pen and pencil, "which if correct would be extremely affecting." Unfortunately, however, for the lovers of the sensational, these pictures are not "correct," but are based on a false assumption which grew up out of a desire to heap contumely on Bunyan's enemies by exaggerating the severity of his protracted, but by no means harsh imprisonment.

Being arrested by the warrant of a county magistrate for a county offence, Bunyan's place of incarceration was naturally the county gaol. There he undoubtedly passed the twelve years of his captivity, and there the royal warrant for his release found him "a prisoner in the common gaol for our county of Bedford." But though far different from the pictures which writers, desirous of exhibiting the sufferings of the Puritan confessor in the most telling form, have drawn—if not "a damp and dreary cell" into which "a narrow chink admits a few scanty rays of light to render visible the prisoner, pale and emaciated, seated on the humid earth, pursuing his daily task to earn the morsel which prolongs his existence and his confinement together,"—"the common gaol" of Bedford must have been a sufficiently strait and unwholesome abode, especially for one, like the travelling tinker, accustomed to spend the greater part of his days in the open-air in unrestricted freedom.

Prisons in those days, and indeed long afterwards, were, at their best, foul, dark, miserable places. A century later Howard found Bedford gaol, though better than some, in what would now be justly deemed a disgraceful condition. One who visited Bunyan during his confinement speaks of it as "an uncomfortable and close prison." Bunyan however himself, in the narrative of his imprisonment, makes no complaint of it, nor do we hear of his health having in any way suffered from the conditions of his confinement, as was the case with not a few of his fellow-sufferers for the sake of religion in other English gaols, some of them even unto death. Bad as it must have been to be a prisoner, as far as his own testimony goes, there is no evidence that his imprisonment, though varying in its strictness with his various gaolers, was aggravated by any special severity; and, as Mr. Froude has said, "it is unlikely that at any time he was made to suffer any greater hardships than were absolutely inevitable."

The arrest of one whose work as a preacher had been a blessing to so many, was not at once tamely acquiesced in by the religious body to which he belonged. A few days after Bunyan's committal to gaol, some of "the brethren" applied to Mr. Crompton, a young magistrate at Elstow, to bail him out, offering the required security for his appearance at the Quarter Sessions. The magistrate was at first disposed to accept the bail; but being a young man, new in his office, and thinking it possible that there might be more against Bunyan than the "mittimus" expressed, he was afraid of compromising himself by letting him go at large. His refusal, though it sent him back to prison, was received by Bunyan with his usual calm trust in God's overruling providence.

"I was not at all daunted, but rather glad, and saw evidently that the Lord had heard me." Before he set out for the justice's house, he tells us he had committed the whole event to God's ordering, with the prayer that "if he might do more good by being at liberty than in prison," the bail might be accepted, "but if not, that His will might be done." In the failure of his friends' good offices he saw an answer to his prayer, encouraging the hope that the untoward event, which deprived them of his personal ministrations, "might be an awaking to the saints in the country," and while "the slender answer of the justice," which sent him back to his prison, stirred something akin to contempt, his soul was full of gladness. "Verily I did meet my God sweetly again, comforting of me, and satisfying of me, that it was His will and mind that I should be there." The sense that he was being conformed to the image of his great Master was a stay to his soul. "This word," he continues, "did drop in upon my heart with some life, for he knew that 'for envy they had delivered him.'"

Seven weeks after his committal, early in January, 1661, the Quarter Sessions came on, and "John Bunyan, of the town of Bedford, labourer," was indicted in the customary form for having "devilishly and perniciously abstained from coming to church to hear Divine Service," and as "a common upholder of several unlawful meetings and conventions, to the great disturbance and distraction of the good subjects of the kingdom." The chairman of the bench was the brutal and blustering Sir John Keeling, the prototype of Bunyan's Lord Hategood in Faithful's trial at Vanity Fair, who afterwards, by his base subserviency to an infamous government, climbed to the Lord Chief Justice's seat, over the head of Sir Matthew Hale.

Keeling had suffered much from the Puritans during the great Rebellion, when, according to Clarendon, he was "always in gaol," and was by no means disposed to deal leniently with an offender of that persuasion. His brethren of the bench were country gentlemen hating Puritanism from their heart, and eager for retaliation for the wrongs it had wrought them. From such a bench, even if Bunyan had been less uncompromising, no leniency was to be anticipated. But Bunyan's attitude forbade any leniency.

As the law stood he had indisputably broken it, and he expressed his determination, respectfully but firmly, to take the first opportunity of breaking it again. "I told them that if I was let out of prison today I would preach the gospel again to-morrow by the help of God." We may dislike the tone adopted by the magistrates towards the prisoner; we may condemn it as overbearing and contemptuous; we may smile at Keeling's expositions of Scripture and his stock arguments against unauthorized prayer and preaching, though we may charitably believe that Bunyan misunderstood him when he makes him say that "the Book of Common Prayer had been ever since the apostles' time"; we may think that the prisoner, in his "canting pedlar's French," as Keeling called it, had the better of his judges in knowledge of the Bible, in Christian charity, as well as in dignity and in common sense, and that they showed their wisdom in silencing him in court—"Let him speak no further," said one of them, "he will do harm,"—since they could not answer him more convincingly: but his legal offence was clear. He confessed to the indictment, if not in express terms, yet virtually. He and his friends had held "many meetings together, both to pray to God and to exhort one another. I confessed myself guilty no otherwise."

Such meetings were forbidden by the law, which it was the duty of the justices to administer, and they had no choice whether they would convict or no. Perhaps they were not sorry they had no such choice. Bunyan was a most "impracticable" prisoner, and as Mr. Froude says, the "magistrates being but unregenerate mortals may be pardoned if they found him provoking." The sentence necessarily followed. It was pronounced, not, we are sure reluctantly, by Keeling, in the terms of the Act. "He was to go back to prison for three months. If at three months' end he still refused to go to church to hear Divine service and leave his preaching, he was to be banished the realm,"—in modern language "transported," and if "he came back again without special royal license," he must "stretch by the neck for it."

"This," said Keeling, "I tell you plainly." Bunyan's reply that "as to that matter he was at a point with the judge," for "that he would repeat the offence the first time he could," provoked a rejoinder from one of the bench, and the unseemly wrangling might have been still further prolonged, had it not been stopped by the gaoler, who "pulling him away to be gone," had him back to prison, where he says, and "blesses the Lord Jesus Christ for it," his heart was as "sweetly refreshed" in returning to it as it had "been during his examination. So that I find Christ's words more than bare trifles, where He saith, He will give a mouth and wisdom, even such as all the adversaries shall not gainsay or resist. And that His peace no man can take from us."

The magistrates, however, though not unnaturally irritated by what seemed to them Bunyan's unreasonable obstinacy, were not desirous to push matters to extremity. The three months named in his sentence, at the expiration of which he was either to conform or be banished the realm, were fast drawing to an end, without any sign of submission on his part. As a last resort Mr. Cobb, the Clerk of the Peace, was sent to try what calm and friendly reasoning might effect. Cobb, who evidently knew Bunyan personally, did his best, as a kind-hearted, sensible man, to bring him to reason. Cobb did not profess to be "a man that could dispute," and Bunyan had the better of him in argument. His position, however, was unassailable.

The recent insurrection of Venner and his Fifth Monarchy men, he said, had shown the danger to the public peace there was in allowing fanatical gatherings to assemble unchecked. Bunyan, whose loyalty was unquestioned, must acknowledge the prudence of suppressing meetings which, however good their ostensible aim, might issue in nothing less than the ruin of the kingdom and commonwealth. Bunyan had confessed his readiness to obey the apostolic precept by submitting himself to the king as supreme.

The king forbade the holding of private meetings, which, under colour of religion, might be prejudicial to the State. Why then did he not submit? This need not hinder him from doing good in a neighbourly way. He might continue to use his gifts and exhort his neighbours in private discourse, provided he did not bring people together in public assemblies. The law did not abridge him of this liberty. Why should he stand so strictly on public meetings? Or why should he not come to church and hear? Was his gift so far above that of others that he could learn of no one? If he could not be persuaded, the judges were resolved to prosecute the law against him. He would be sent away beyond the seas to Spain or Constantinople—either Cobb's or Bunyan's colonial geography was rather at fault here—or some other remote part of the world, and what good could he do to his friends then?

"Neighbour Bunyan" had better consider these things seriously before the Quarter Session, and be ruled by good advice. The gaoler here put in his word in support of Cobb's arguments: "Indeed, sir, I hope he will be ruled." But all Cobb's friendly reasonings and expostulations were ineffectual to bend Bunyan's sturdy will. He would yield to no-one in his loyalty to his sovereign, and his readiness to obey the law.

But, he said, with a hairsplitting casuistry he would have indignantly condemned in others, the law provided two ways of obeying, "one to obey actively, and if his conscience forbad that, then to obey passively; to lie down and suffer whatever they might do to him." The Clerk of the Peace saw that it was no use to prolong the argument any further. "At this," writes Bunyan, "he sat down, and said no more; which, when he had done, I did thank him for his civil and meek discoursing with me; and so we parted: O that we might meet in heaven!" The Coronation which took place very soon after this interview, April 13, 1661, afforded a prospect of release without unworthy submission. The customary proclamation, which allowed prisoners under sentence for any offence short of felony to sue out a pardon for twelve months from that date, suspended the execution of the sentence of banishment and gave a hope that the prison doors might be opened for him.

The local authorities taking no steps to enable him to profit by the royal clemency, by inserting his name in the list of pardonable offenders, his second wife, Elizabeth, travelled up to London,—no slight venture for a young woman not so long raised from the sick bed on which the first news of her husband's arrest had laid her,—and with dauntless courage made her way to the House of Lords, where she presented her petition to one of the peers, whom she calls Lord Barkwood, but whom unfortunately we cannot now identify. He treated her kindly, and showed her petition to other peers, who appear to have been acquainted with the circumstances of Bunyan's case. They replied that the matter was beyond their province, and that the question of her husband's release was committed to the judges at the next assizes. These assizes were held at Bedford in the following August.

The judges of the circuit were Twisden and Sir Matthew Hale. From the latter—the friend of Richard Baxter, who, as Burnet records, took great care to "cover the Nonconformists, whom he thought too hardly used, all he could from the seventies some designed; and discouraged those who were inclined to stretch the laws too much against them"— Bunyan's case would be certain to meet with sympathetic consideration. But being set to administer the law, not according to his private wishes, but according to its letter and its spirit, he was powerless to relieve him. Three several times did Bunyan's noble-hearted wife present her husband's petition that he might be heard, and his case taken impartially into consideration.

But the law forbad what Burnet calls Sir Matthew Hale's "tender and compassionate nature" to have free exercise. He "received the petition very mildly at her hand, telling her that he would do her and her husband the best good he could; but he feared he could do none." His brother judge's reception of her petition was very different. Having thrown it into the coach, Twisden "snapt her up," telling her, what after all was no more than the truth, that her husband was a convicted person, and could not be released unless he would promise to obey the law and abstain from preaching. On this the High Sheriff, Edmund Wylde, of Houghton Conquest, spoke kindly to the poor woman, and encouraged her to make a fresh application to the judges before they left the town. So she made her way, "with abashed face and trembling heart," to the large chamber at the Old Swan Inn at the Bridge Foot, where the two judges were receiving a large number of the justices of the peace and other gentry of the county.

Addressing Sir Matthew Hale she said, "My lord, I make bold to come again to your lordship to know what may be done with my husband." Hale received her with the same gentleness as before, repeated what he had said previously, that as her husband had been legally convicted, and his conviction was recorded, unless there was something to undo that he could do her no good. Twisden, on the other hand, got violently angry, charged her brutally with making poverty her cloak, told her that her husband was a breaker of the peace, whose doctrine was the doctrine of the devil, and that he ran up and down and did harm, while he was better maintained by his preaching than by following his tinker's craft. At last he waxed so violent that "withal she thought he would have struck her."

In the midst of all his coarse abuse, however, Twisden hit the mark when he asked: "What! you think we can do what we list?" And when we find Hale, confessedly the soundest lawyer of the time, whose sympathies were all with the prisoner, after calling for the Statute Book, thus summing up the matter: "I am sorry, woman, that I can do thee no good. Thou must do one of these three things, viz., either apply thyself to the king, or sue out his pardon, or get a writ of error," which last, he told her, would be the cheapest course—we may feel sure that Bunyan's Petition was not granted because it could not be granted legally.

The blame of his continued imprisonment lay, if anywhere, with the law, not with its administrators. This is not always borne in mind as it ought to be. As Mr. Froude remarks, "Persons often choose to forget that judges are sworn to administer the law which they find, and rail at them as if the sentences which they are obliged by their oath to pass were their own personal acts." It is not surprising that Elizabeth Bunyan was unable to draw this distinction, and that she left the Swan chamber in tears, not, however, so much at what she thought the judges' "hardheartedness to her and her husband," as at the thought of "the sad account such poor creatures would have to give" hereafter, for what she deemed their "opposition to Christ and His gospel."

No steps seem to have been taken by Bunyan's wife, or any of his influential friends, to carry out either of the expedients named by Hale. It may have been that the money needed was not forthcoming, or, what Southey remarks is "quite probable,"—"because it is certain that Bunyan, thinking himself in conscience bound to preach in defiance of the law, would soon have made his case worse than it then was."

At the next assizes, which were held in January, 1662, Bunyan again made strenuous efforts to get his name put on the calendar of felons, that he might have a regular trial before the king's judges and be able to plead his cause in person. This, however, was effectually thwarted by the unfriendly influence of the county magistrates by whom he had been committed, and the Clerk of the Peace, Mr. Cobb, who having failed in his kindly meant attempt to induce "Neighbour Bunyan" to conform, had turned bitterly against him and become one of his chief enemies. "Thus," writes Bunyan, "was I hindered and prevented at that time also from appearing before the judge, and left in prison." Of this prison, the county gaol of Bedford, he remained an inmate, with one, short interval in 1666, for the next twelve years, till his release by order of the Privy Council, May 17, 1672.

Chapter 6

The exaggeration of the severity of Bunyan's imprisonment long current, now that the facts are better known, has led, by a very intelligible reaction, to an undue depreciation of it. Mr. Froude thinks that his incarceration was "intended to be little more than nominal," and was really meant in kindness by the authorities who "respected his character," as the best means of preventing him from getting himself into greater trouble by "repeating an offence that would compel them to adopt harsh measures which they were earnestly trying to avoid."

If convicted again he must be transported, and "they were unwilling to drive him out of the country." It is, however, to be feared that it was no such kind consideration for the tinker-preacher which kept the prison doors closed on Bunyan. To the justices he was simply an obstinate law-breaker, who must be kept in prison as long as he refused compliance with the Act. If he rotted in gaol, as so many of his fellow sufferers for conscience' sake did in those unhappy times, it was no concern of theirs. He and his stubbornness would be alone to blame.

It is certainly true that during a portion of his captivity, Bunyan, in Dr. Brown's words, "had an amount of liberty which in the case of a prisoner nowadays would be simply impossible." But the mistake has been made of extending to the whole period an indulgence which belonged only to a part, and that a very limited part of it. When we are told that Bunyan was treated as a prisoner at large, and like one "on parole," free to come and go as he pleased, even as far as London, we must remember that Bunyan's own words expressly restrict this indulgence to the six months between the Autumn Assizes of 1661 and the Spring Assizes of 1662. "Between these two assizes," he says, "I had by my jailer some liberty granted me more than at the first." This liberty was certainly of the largest kind consistent with his character of a prisoner. The church books show that he was occasionally present at their meetings, and was employed on the business of the congregation. Nay, even his preaching, which was the cause of his imprisonment, was not forbidden.

"I followed," he says, writing of this period, "my wonted course of preaching, taking all occasions that were put into my hand to visit the people of God." But this indulgence was very brief and was brought sharply to an end. It was plainly irregular, and depended on the connivance of his jailer. We cannot be surprised that when it came to the magistrates' ears—"my enemies," Bunyan rather unworthily calls them—they were seriously displeased.

Confounding Bunyan with the Fifth Monarchy men and other turbulent sectaries, they imagined that his visits to London had a political object, "to plot, and raise division, and make insurrections," which, he honestly adds, "God knows was a slander." The jailer was all but "cast out of his place," and threatened with an indictment for breach of trust, while his own liberty was so seriously "straitened" that he was prohibited even "to look out at the door." The last time Bunyan's name appears as present at a church meeting is October 28, 1661, nor do we see it again till October 9, 1668, only four years before his twelve years term of imprisonment expired.

But though his imprisonment was not so severe, nor his prison quite so narrow and wretched as some word-painters have described them, during the greater part of the time his condition was a dreary and painful one, especially when spent, as it sometimes was, "under cruel and oppressive jailers." The enforced separation from his wife and children, especially his tenderly loved blind daughter, Mary, was a continually renewed anguish to his loving heart.

"The parting with them," he writes, "hath often been to me as pulling the flesh from the bones; and that not only because I am somewhat too fond of these great mercies, but also because I should often have brought to my mind the many hardships, miseries, and wants my poor family was like to meet with, should I be taken from them; especially my poor blind child, who lay nearer to my heart than all beside. Poor child, thought I, thou must be beaten, thou must beg, thou must suffer hunger, cold, nakedness, and a thousand calamities, though I cannot now endure the wind should blow on thee. O, the thoughts of the hardships my blind one might go under would break my heart to pieces." He seemed to himself like a man pulling down his house on his wife and children's head, and yet he felt, "I must do it; O, I must do it." He was also, he tells us, at one time, being but "a young prisoner," greatly troubled by the thoughts that "for aught he could tell," his "imprisonment might end at the gallows," not so much that he dreaded death as that he was apprehensive that when it came to the point, even if he made "a scrabbling shift to clamber up the ladder," he might play the coward and so do discredit to the cause of religion.

"I was ashamed to die with a pale face and tottering knees for such a cause as this." The belief that his imprisonment might be terminated by death on the scaffold, however groundless, evidently weighed long on his mind. The closing sentences of his third prison book, "Christian Behaviour," published in 1663, the second year of his durance, clearly point to such an expectation. "Thus have I in few words written to you before I die,... not knowing the shortness of my life, nor the hindrances that hereafter I may have of serving my God and you." The ladder of his apprehensions was, as Mr. Froude has said, "an imaginary ladder," but it was very real to Bunyan.

"Oft I was as if I was on the ladder with a rope about my neck." The thought of it, as his autobiography shows, caused him some of his deepest searchings of heart, and noblest ventures of faith. He was content to suffer by the hangman's hand if thus he might have an opportunity of addressing the crowd that he thought would come to see him die. "And if it must be so, if God will but convert one soul by my very last words, I shall not count my life thrown away or lost."

And even when hours of darkness came over his soul, and he was tempted to question the reality of his Christian profession, and to doubt whether God would give him comfort at the hour of death, he stayed himself up with such bold words as these. "I was bound, but He was free. Yea, 'twas my duty to stand to His word whether He would ever look on me or no, or save me at the last. If God doth not come in, thought I, I will leap off the ladder even blindfold into Eternity, sink or swim, come heaven, come hell. Lord Jesus, if Thou wilt catch me, do. If not, I will venture for Thy name."

Bunyan being precluded by his imprisonment from carrying on his brazier's craft for the support of his wife and family, and his active spirit craving occupation, he got himself taught how to make "long tagged laces," "many hundred gross" of which, we are told by one who first formed his acquaintance in prison, he made during his captivity, for "his own and his family's necessities." "While his hands were thus busied," writes Lord Macaulay, "he had often employment for his mind and for his lips." "Though a prisoner he was a preacher still." As with St. Paul in his Roman chains, "the word of God was not bound."

The prisoners for conscience' sake, who like him, from time to time, were cooped up in Bedford gaol, including several of his brother ministers and some of his old friends among the leading members of his own little church, furnished a numerous and sympathetic congregation. At one time a body of some sixty, who had met for worship at night in a neighbouring wood, were marched off to gaol, with their minister at their head. But while all about him was in confusion, his spirit maintained its even calm, and he could at once speak the words of strength and comfort that were needed. In the midst of the hurry which so many "newcomers occasioned," writes the friend to whom we are indebted for the details of his prison life, "I have heard Mr. Bunyan both preach and pray with that mighty spirit of faith and plerophory of Divine assistance that has made me stand and wonder."

These sermons addressed to his fellow prisoners supplied, in many cases, the first outlines of the books which, in rapid succession, flowed from his pen during the earlier years of his imprisonment, relieving the otherwise insupportable tedium of his close confinement. Bunyan himself tells us that this was the case with regard to his "Holy City," the first idea of which was borne in upon his mind when addressing "his brethren in the prison chamber," nor can we doubt that the case was the same with other works of his.

To these we shall hereafter return. Nor was it his fellow prisoners only who profited by his counsels. In his "Life and Death of Mr. Badman," he gives us a story of a woman who came to him when he was in prison, to confess how she had robbed her master, and to ask his help. Hers was probably a representative case. The time spared from his handicraft, and not employed in religious counsel and exhortation, was given to study and composition. For this his confinement secured him the leisure which otherwise he would have looked for in vain.

The few books he possessed he studied indefatigably. His library was, at least at one period, a very limited one,—"the least and the best library," writes a friend who visited him in prison, "that I ever saw, consisting only of two books—the Bible, and Foxe's 'Book of Martyrs.'" "But with these two books," writes Mr. Froude, "he had no cause to complain of intellectual destitution." Bunyan's mode of composition, though certainly exceedingly rapid,—thoughts succeeding one another with a quickness akin to inspiration,—was anything but careless. The "limæ labor" with him was unsparing. It was, he tells us, "first with doing, and then with undoing, and after that with doing again," that his books were brought to completion, and became what they are, a mine of Evangelical Calvinism of the richest ore, entirely free from the narrow dogmatism and harsh predestinarianism of the great Genevan divine; books which for clearness of thought, lucidity of arrangement, felicity of language, rich even if sometimes homely force of illustration, and earnestness of piety have never been surpassed.

Bunyan's prison life when the first bitterness of it was past, and habit had done away with its strangeness, was a quiet and it would seem, not an unhappy one. A manly self-respect bore him up and forbade his dwelling on the darker features of his position, or thinking or speaking harshly of the authors of his durance. "He was," writes one who saw him at this time, "mild and affable in conversation; not given to loquacity or to much discourse unless some urgent occasion required. It was observed he never spoke of himself or his parents, but seemed low in his own eyes. He was never heard to reproach or revile, whatever injury he received, but rather rebuked those who did so. He managed all things with such exactness as if he had made it his study not to give offence."

According to his earliest biographer, Charles Doe, in 1666, the year of the Fire of London, after Bunyan had lain six years in Bedford gaol, "by the intercession of some interest or power that took pity on his sufferings," he enjoyed a short interval of liberty. Who these friends and sympathisers were is not mentioned, and it would be vain to conjecture. This period of freedom, however, was very short. He at once resumed his old work of preaching, against which the laws had become even more stringent during his imprisonment, and was apprehended at a meeting just as he was about to preach a sermon. He had given out his text, "Dost thou believe on the Son of God?" (John 9:35), and was standing with his open Bible in his hand, when the constable came in to take him.

Bunyan fixed his eyes on the man, who turned pale, let go his hold, and drew back, while Bunyan exclaimed, "See how this man trembles at the word of God!" This is all we know of his second arrest, and even this little is somewhat doubtful. The time, the place, the circumstances, are as provokingly vague as much else of Bunyan's life. The fact, however, is certain. Bunyan returned to Bedford gaol, where he spent another six years, until the issuing of the "Declaration of Indulgence" early in 1672 opened the long-closed doors, and he walked out a free man, and with what he valued far more than personal liberty, freedom to deliver Christ's message as he understood it himself, none making him afraid, and to declare to his brother sinners what their Saviour had done for them, and what he expected them to do that they might obtain the salvation He died to win.

From some unknown cause, perhaps the depressing effect of protracted confinement, during this second six years Bunyan's pen was far less prolific than during the former period. Only two of his books are dated in these years. The last of these, "A Defence of the Doctrine of Justification by Faith," a reply to a work of Edward Fowler, afterwards Bishop of Gloucester, the rector of Northill, was written in hot haste immediately before his release, and issued from the press contemporaneously with it, the prospect of liberty apparently breathing new life into his wearied soul.

When once Bunyan became a free man again, his pen recovered its former copiousness of production, and the works by which he has been immortalized, "The Pilgrim's Progress"—which has been erroneously ascribed to Bunyan's twelve years' imprisonment—and its sequel, "The Holy War," and the "Life and Death of Mr. Badman," and a host of more strictly theological works, followed one another in rapid succession.

Bunyan's second term of imprisonment was certainly less severe than that which preceded it. At its commencement we learn that, like Joseph in Egypt, he found favour in his jailer's eyes, who "took such pity of his rigorous suffering, that he put all care and trust into his hands." Towards the close of his imprisonment its rigour was still further relaxed. The Bedford church book begins its record again in 1688, after an interval of ominous silence of five years, when the persecution was at the hottest. In its earliest entries we find Bunyan's name, which occurs repeatedly up to the date of his final release in 1672.

Not one of these notices gives the slightest allusion of his being a prisoner. He is deputed with others to visit and remonstrate with backsliding brethren, and fulfil other commissions on behalf of the congregation, as if he were in the full enjoyment of his liberty. This was in the two years' interval between the expiration of the Conventicle Act, March 2, 1667-8, and the passing of the new Act, styled by Marvell, "the quintessence of arbitrary malice," April 11, 1670.

After a few months of hot persecution, when a disgraceful system of espionage was set on foot and the vilest wretches drove a lucrative trade as spies on "meetingers," the severity greatly lessened. Charles II. was already meditating the issuing of a Declaration of Indulgence, and signified his disapprobation of the "forceable courses" in which, "the sad experience of twelve years" showed, there was "very little fruit." One of the first and most notable consequences of this change of policy was Bunyan's release.

Mr. Offor's patient researches in the State Paper Office have proved that the Quakers, than whom no class of sectaries had suffered more severely from the persecuting edicts of the Crown, were mainly instrumental in throwing open the prison doors to those who, like Bunyan, were in bonds for the sake of their religion. Gratitude to John Groves, the Quaker mate of Tattersall's fishing boat, in which Charles had escaped to France after the battle of Worcester, had something, and the untiring advocacy of George Whitehead, the Quaker, had still more, to do with this act of royal clemency.

We can readily believe that the good-natured Charles was not sorry to have an opportunity of evidencing his sense of former services rendered at a time of his greatest extremity. But the main cause lay much deeper, and is connected with what Lord Macaulay justly styles "one of the worst acts of one of the worst governments that England has ever seen"—that of the Cabal. Our national honour was at its lowest ebb. Charles had just concluded the profligate Treaty of Dover, by which, in return for the "protection" he sought from the French king, he declared himself a Roman Catholic at heart, and bound himself to take the first opportunity of "changing the present state of religion in England for a better," and restoring the authority of the Pope.

The announcement of his conversion Charles found it convenient to postpone. Nor could the other part of his engagement be safely carried into effect at once. It called for secret and cautious preparation. But to pave the way for it, by an unconstitutional exercise of his prerogative he issued a Declaration of Indulgence which suspended all penal laws against "whatever sort of Nonconformists or Recusants." The latter were evidently the real object of the indulgence; the former class were only introduced the better to cloke his infamous design. Toleration, however, was thus at last secured, and the long-oppressed Nonconformists hastened to profit by it.

"Ministers returned," writes Mr. J. R. Green, "after years of banishment, to their homes and their flocks. Chapels were re-opened. The gaols were emptied. Men were set free to worship God after their own fashion. John Bunyan left the prison which had for twelve years been his home." More than three thousand licenses to preach were at once issued. One of the earliest of these, dated May 9, 1672, four months before his formal pardon under the Great Seal, was granted to Bunyan, who in the preceding January had been chosen their minister by the little congregation at Bedford, and "giving himself up to serve Christ and His Church in that charge, had received of the elders the right hand of fellowship." The place licensed for the exercise of Bunyan's ministry was a barn standing in an orchard, once forming part of the Castle Moat, which one of the congregation, Josias Roughead, acting for the members of his church, had purchased.

The license bears date May 9, 1672. This primitive place of worship, in which Bunyan preached regularly till his death, was pulled down in 1707, when a "three-ridged meeting-house" was erected in its place. This in its turn gave way, in 1849, to the existing more seemly chapel, to which the present Duke of Bedford, in 1876, presented a pair of noble bronze doors bearing scenes, in high relief, from "The Pilgrim's Progress," the work of Mr. Frederick Thrupp. In the vestry are preserved Bunyan's chair, and other relics of the man who has made the name of Bedford famous to the whole civilized world.

Chapter 7

Mr. Green has observed that Bunyan "found compensation for the narrow bounds of his prison in the wonderful activity of his pen. Tracts, controversial treatises, poems, meditations, his 'Grace Abounding,' and his 'Holy War,' followed each other in quick succession." Bunyan's literary fertility in the earlier half of his imprisonment was indeed amazing. Even if, as seems almost certain, we have been hitherto in error in assigning the First Part of "The Pilgrim's Progress" to this period, while the "Holy War" certainly belongs to a later, the works which had their birth in Bedford Gaol during the first six years of his confinement, are of themselves sufficient to make the reputation of any ordinary writer. As has been already remarked, for some unexplained cause, Bunyan's gifts as an author were much more sparingly called into exercise during the second half of his captivity. Only two works appear to have been written between 1666 and his release in 1672.

Mr. Green has spoken of "poems" as among the products of Bunyan's pen during this period. The compositions in verse belonging to this epoch, of which there are several, hardly deserve to be dignified with so high a title. At no part of his life had Bunyan much title to be called a poet. He did not aspire beyond the rank of a versifier, who clothed his thoughts in rhyme or metre instead of the more congenial prose, partly for the pleasure of the exercise, partly because he knew by experience that the lessons he wished to inculcate were more likely to be remembered in that form. Mr. Froude, who takes a higher estimate of Bunyan's verse than is commonly held, remarks that though it is the fashion to apply the epithet of "doggerel" to it, the "sincere and rational meaning" which pervades his compositions renders such an epithet improper. "His ear for rhythm," he continues, "though less true than in his prose, is seldom wholly at fault, and whether in prose or verse, he had the superlative merit that he could never write nonsense."

Bunyan's earliest prison work, entitled "Profitable Meditations," was in verse, and neither this nor his later metrical ventures before his release—his "Four Last Things," his "Ebal and Gerizim," and his "Prison Meditations"—can be said to show much poetical power. At best he is a mere rhymester, to whom rhyme and metre, even when self-chosen, were as uncongenial accoutrements "as Saul's armour was to David." The first-named book, which is entitled a "Conference between Christ and a Sinner," in the form of a poetical dialogue, according to Dr. Brown has "small literary merit of any sort."

The others do not deserve much higher commendation. There is an individuality about the "Prison Meditations" which imparts to it a personal interest, which is entirely wanting in the other two works, which may be characterized as metrical sermons, couched in verse of the Sternhold and Hopkins type. A specimen or two will suffice. The "Four Last Things" thus opens:—

> These lines I at this time present
> To all that will them heed,
> Wherein I show to what intent
> God saith, 'Convert with speed.'
> For these four things come on apace,
> Which we should know full well,
> Both death and judgment, and, in place
> Next to them, heaven and hell.

The following lines are from "Ebal and Gerizim":—

> Thou art like one that hangeth by a thread
> Over the mouth of hell, as one half dead;
> And oh, how soon this thread may broken be,

Or cut by death, is yet unknown to thee.
But sure it is if all the weight of sin,
And all that Satan too hath doing been
Or yet can do, can break this crazy thread,
'Twill not be long before among the dead
Thou tumble do, as linkèd fast in chains,
With them to wait in fear for future pains.

The poetical effusion entitled "Prison Meditations" does not in any way rise above the prosaic level of its predecessors. But it can be read with less weariness from the picture it presents of Bunyan's prison life, and of the courageous faith which sustained him. Some unnamed friend, it would appear, fearing he might flinch, had written him a letter counselling him to keep "his head above the flood."

Bunyan replied in seventy stanzas in ballad measure, thanking his correspondent for his good advice, of which he confesses he stood in need, and which he takes it kindly of him to send, even though his feet stand upon Mount Zion, and the gaol is to him like a hill from which he could see beyond this world, and take his fill of the blessedness of that which remains for the Christian. Though in bonds his mind is free, and can wander where it will.

For though men keep my outward man
Within their locks and bars,
Yet by the faith of Christ, I can
Mount higher than the stars.

Meanwhile his captivity is sweetened by the thought of what it was that brought him there:—

I here am very much refreshed
To think, when I was out,
I preachèd life, and peace, and rest,

To sinners round about.

My business then was souls to save
By preaching grace and faith,
Of which the comfort now I have
And have it shall till death.

That was the work I was about
When hands on me they laid.
'Twas this for which they plucked me out
And vilely to me said,

'You heretic, deceiver, come,
To prison you must go,
You preach abroad, and keep not home,
You are the Church's foe.'

Wherefore to prison they me sent,
Where to this day I lie,
And can with very much content
For my profession die.

The prison very sweet to me
Hath been since I came here,
And so would also hanging be
If God would there appear.

To them that here for evil lie
The place is comfortless;
But not to me, because that I
Lie here for righteousness.

The truth and I were both here cast

> Together, and we do
> Lie arm in arm, and so hold fast
> Each other, this is true.
>
> Who now dare say we throw away
> Our goods or liberty,
> When God's most holy Word doth say
> We gain thus much thereby?

It will be seen that though Bunyan's verses are certainly not high-class poetry, they are very far removed from doggerel. Nothing indeed that Bunyan ever wrote, however rugged the rhymes and limping the metre, can be so stigmatized. The rude scribblings on the margins of the copy of the "Book of Martyrs," which bears Bunyan's signature on the title-pages, though regarded by Southey as "undoubtedly" his, certainly came from a later and must less instructed pen. And as he advanced in his literary career, his claim to the title of a poet, though never of the highest, was much strengthened.

The verses which diversify the narrative in the Second Part of "The Pilgrim's Progress" are decidedly superior to those in the First Part, and some are of high excellence. Who is ignorant of the charming little song of the Shepherd Boy in the Valley of Humiliation, "in very mean clothes, but with a very fresh and well-favoured countenance, and wearing more of the herb called Heartsease in his bosom than he that is clad in silk and velvet?"—

> He that is down need fear no fall;
> He that is low, no pride;
> He that is humble, ever shall
> Have God to be his guide.
>
> I am content with what I have,
> Little be it or much,

And, Lord, contentment still I crave,
Because Thou savest such.

Fulness to such a burden is
That go on Pilgrimage,
Here little, and hereafter Bliss
Is best from age to age.

Bunyan reaches a still higher flight in Valiant-for-Truth's song, later on, the Shakesperian ring of which recalls Amiens' in "As You Like It,"

Under the greenwood tree,
Who loves to lie with me...
Come hither, come hither,

and has led some to question whether it can be Bunyan's own. The resemblance, as Mr. Froude remarks, is "too near to be accidental." "Perhaps he may have heard the lines, and the rhymes may have clung to him without his knowing whence they came."

Who would true Valour see,
Let him come hither,
One here will constant be,
Come wind, come weather.
There's no discouragement
Shall make him once relent
His first avowed intent
To be a Pilgrim.

Who so beset him round
With dismal stories,
Do but themselves confound
His strength the more is.

No lion can him fright,
He'll with a giant fight,
But he will have a right
To be a Pilgrim.

Hobgoblin nor foul fiend
Can daunt his spirit,
He knows he at the end
Shall life inherit.
Then fancies fly away
He'll fear not what men say,
He'll labour night and day
To be a Pilgrim.

All readers of "The Pilgrim's Progress" and "The Holy War" are familiar with the long metrical compositions giving the history of these works by which they are prefaced and the latter work is closed. No more characteristic examples of Bunyan's muse can be found. They show his excellent command of his native tongue in racy vernacular, homely but never vulgar, and his power of expressing his meaning "with sharp defined outlines and without the waste of a word."

Take this account of his perplexity, when the First Part of his "Pilgrim's Progress" was finished, whether it should be given to the world or no, and the characteristic decision with which he settled the question for himself:—

Well, when I had then put mine ends together,
I show'd them others that I might see whether
They would condemn them, or them justify;
And some said Let them live; some, Let them die.
Some said, John, print it; others said, Not so;
Some said it might do good; others said No.
Now was I in a strait, and did not see

> Which was the best thing to be done by me;
> At last I thought since you are thus divided
> I print it will; and so the case decided;

or the lines in which he introduces the Second Part of the Pilgrim to the readers of the former part:—

> Go now, my little Book, to every place
> Where my first Pilgrim hath but shown his face:
> Call at their door: If any say, 'Who's there?'
> Then answer that Christiana is here.
> If they bid thee come in, then enter thou
> With all thy boys. And then, as thou knowest how,
> Tell who they are, also from whence they came;
> Perhaps they'll know them by their looks or name.
> But if they should not, ask them yet again
> If formerly they did not entertain
> One Christian, a pilgrim. If they say
> They did, and were delighted in his way:
> Then let them know that these related are
> Unto him, yea, his wife and children are.
> Tell them that they have left their house and home,
> Are turned Pilgrims, seek a world to come;
> That they have met with hardships on the way,
> That they do meet with troubles night and day.

How racy, even if the lines are a little halting, is the defence of the genuineness of his Pilgrim in "The Advertisement to the Reader" at the end of "The Holy War."

> Some say the Pilgrim's Progress is not mine,
> Insinuating as if I would shine
> In name or fame by the worth of another,

> Like some made rich by robbing of their brother;
> Or that so fond I am of being sire
> I'll father bastards; or if need require,
> I'll tell a lie or print to get applause.
> I scorn it. John such dirt-heap never was
> Since God converted him...
> Witness my name, if anagram'd to thee
> The letters make Nu hony in a B.
> IOHN BUNYAN."

How full of life and vigour his sketch of the beleaguerment and deliverance of "Mansoul," as a picture of his own spiritual experience, in the introductory verses to "The Holy War"!—

> For my part I, myself, was in the town,
> Both when 'twas set up, and when pulling down;
> I saw Diabolus in possession,
> And Mansoul also under his oppression.
> Yes, I was there when she crowned him for lord,
> And to him did submit with one accord.
> When Mansoul trampled upon things divine,
> And wallowed in filth as doth a swine,
> When she betook herself unto her arms,
> Fought her Emmanuel, despised his charms:
> Then I was there, and did rejoice to see
> Diabolus and Mansoul so agree.
> I saw the prince's armed men come down
> By troops, by thousands, to besiege the town,
> I saw the captains, heard the trumpets sound,
> And how his forces covered all the ground,
> Yea, how they set themselves in battle array,
> I shall remember to my dying day.

Bunyan's other essays in the domain of poetry need not detain us long. The most considerable of these—at least in bulk—if it be really his, is a version of some portions of the Old and New Testaments: the life of Joseph, the Book of Ruth, the history of Samson, the Book of Jonah, the Sermon on the Mount, and the General Epistle of St. James. The attempt to do the English Bible into verse has been often made and never successfully: in the nature of things success in such a task is impossible, nor can this attempt be regarded as happier than that of others.

Mr. Froude indeed, who undoubtingly accepts their genuineness, is of a different opinion. He styles the "Book of Ruth" and the "History of Joseph" "beautiful idylls," of such high excellence that, "if we found them in the collected works of a poet laureate, we should consider that a difficult task had been accomplished successfully." It would seem almost doubtful whether Mr. Froude can have read the compositions that he commends so largely, and so much beyond their merit. The following specimen, taken haphazard, will show how thoroughly Bunyan or the rhymester, whoever he may be, has overcome what Mr. Froude regards as an almost insuperable difficulty, and has managed to "spoil completely the faultless prose of the English translation":—

> Ruth replied,
> Intreat me not to leave thee or return;
> For where thou goest I'll go, where thou sojourn
> I'll sojourn also—and what people's thine,
> And who thy God, the same shall both be mine.
> Where thou shalt die, there will I die likewise,
> And I'll be buried where thy body lies.
> The Lord do so to me and more if I
> Do leave thee or forsake thee till I die.

The more we read of these poems, not given to the world till twelve years after Bunyan's death, and that by a publisher who was "a repeated offender against the laws of honest dealing," the more we are inclined to agree with Dr. Brown, that the internal evidence of their style renders their genuineness at the least questionable. In the dull prosaic level of these compositions there is certainly no trace of the "force and power" always present in Bunyan's rudest rhymes, still less of the "dash of genius" and the "sparkle of soul" which occasionally discover the hand of a master.

Of the authenticity of Bunyan's "Divine Emblems," originally published three years after his death under the title of "Country Rhymes for Children," there is no question. The internal evidence confirms the external. The book is thoroughly in Bunyan's vein, and in its homely naturalness of imagery recalls the similitudes of the "Interpreter's House," especially those expounded to Christiana and her boys.

As in that "house of imagery" things of the most common sort, the sweeping of a room, the burning of a fire, the drinking of a chicken, a robin with a spider in his mouth, are made the vehicle of religious teaching; so in this "Book for Boys and Girls," a mole burrowing in the ground, a swallow soaring in the air, the cuckoo which can do nothing but utter two notes, a flaming and a blinking candle, or a pound of candles falling to the ground, a boy chasing a butterfly, the cackling of a hen when she has laid her egg, all, to his imaginative mind, set forth some spiritual truth or enforce some wholesome moral lesson. How racy, though homely, are these lines on a Frog!—

> The Frog by nature is but damp and cold,
> Her mouth is large, her belly much will hold,
> She sits somewhat ascending, loves to be
> Croaking in gardens, though unpleasantly.
>
> The hypocrite is like unto this Frog,
> As like as is the puppy to the dog.
> He is of nature cold, his mouth is wide

To prate, and at true goodness to deride.
And though this world is that which he doth love,
He mounts his head as if he lived above.
And though he seeks in churches for to croak,
He neither seeketh Jesus nor His yoke.

There is some real poetry in those on the Cuckoo, though we may be inclined to resent his harsh treatment of our universal favourite:—

Thou booby says't thou nothing but Cuckoo?
The robin and the wren can that outdo.
They to us play thorough their little throats
Not one, but sundry pretty tuneful notes.
But thou hast fellows, some like thee can do
Little but suck our eggs, and sing Cuckoo.

Thy notes do not first welcome in our spring,
Nor dost thou its first tokens to us bring.
Birds less than thee by far like prophets do
Tell us 'tis coming, though not by Cuckoo,
Nor dost thou summer bear away with thee
Though thou a yawling bawling Cuckoo be.
When thou dost cease among us to appear,
Then doth our harvest bravely crown our year.
But thou hast fellows, some like thee can do
Little but suck our eggs, and sing Cuckoo.

Since Cuckoos forward not our early spring
Nor help with notes to bring our harvest in,
And since while here, she only makes a noise
So pleasing unto none as girls and boys,
The Formalist we may compare her to,
For he doth suck our eggs and sing Cuckoo.

A perusal of this little volume with its roughness and quaintness, sometimes grating on the ear but full of strong thought and picturesque images, cannot fail to raise Bunyan's pretensions as a poet. His muse, it is true, as Alexander Smith has said, is a homely one. She is "clad in russet, wears shoes and stockings, has a country accent, and walks along the level Bedfordshire roads." But if the lines are unpolished, "they have pith and sinew, like the talk of a shrewd peasant," with the "strong thought and the knack of the skilled workman who can drive by a single blow the nail home to the head."

During his imprisonment Bunyan's pen was much more fertile in prose than in poetry. Besides his world-famous "Grace Abounding," he produced during the first six years of his gaol life a treatise on prayer, entitled "Praying in the Spirit;" a book on "Christian Behaviour," setting forth with uncompromising plainness the relative duties of husbands and wives, parents and children, masters and servants, by which those who profess a true faith are bound to show forth its reality and power; the "Holy City," an exposition of the vision in the closing chapters of the Book of Revelation, brilliant with picturesque description and rich in suggestive thought, which, he tells us, had its origin in a sermon preached by him to his brethren in bonds in their prison chamber; and a work on the "Resurrection of the Dead and Eternal Judgment."

On these works we may not linger. There is not one of them which is not marked by vigour of thought, clearness of language, accuracy of arrangement, and deep spiritual experience. Nor is there one which does not here and there exhibit specimens of Bunyan's picturesque imaginative power, and his command of forcible and racy language. Each will reward perusal. His work on "Prayer" is couched in the most exalted strain, and is evidently the production of one who by long and agonizing experience had learnt the true nature of prayer, as a pouring out of the soul to God, and a wrestling with Him until the blessing, delayed not denied, is granted. It is, however, unhappily deformed by much ignorant reviling of the Book of Common Prayer. He denounces it as "taken out of the papistical mass-book, the scraps and fragments of some popes, some friars, and I know not what;" and ridicules the order of service it propounds to the worshippers.

"They have the matter and the manner of their prayer at their fingers' ends; they set such a prayer for such a day, and that twenty years before it comes: one for Christmas, another for Easter, and six days after that. They have also bounded how many syllables must be said in every one of them at their public exercises. For each saint's day also they have them ready for the generations yet unborn to say. They can tell you also when you shall kneel, when you shall stand, when you should abide in your seats, when you should go up into the chancel, and what you should do when you come there. All which the apostles came short of, as not being able to compose so profound a manner." This bitter satirical vein in treating of sacred things is unworthy of its author, and degrading to his sense of reverence. It has its excuse in the hard measure he had received from those who were so unwisely endeavouring to force the Prayer Book on a generation which had largely forgotten it. In his mind, the men and the book were identified, and the unchristian behaviour of its advocates blinded his eyes to its merits as a guide to devotion. Bunyan, when denouncing forms in worship, forgot that the same apostle who directs that in our public assemblies everything should be done "to edification," directs also that everything should be done "decently and in order."

By far the most important of these prison works—"The Pilgrim's Progress," belonging, as will be seen, to a later period—is the "Grace Abounding," in which with inimitable earnestness and simplicity Bunyan gives the story of his early life and his religious history. This book, if he had written no other, would stamp Bunyan as one of the greatest masters of the English language of his own or any other age. In graphic delineation of the struggles of a conscience convicted of sin towards a hardly won freedom and peace, the alternations of light and darkness, of hope and despair, which chequered its course, its morbid self-torturing questionings of motive and action, this work of the travelling tinker, as a spiritual history, has never been surpassed.

Its equal can hardly be found, save perhaps in the "Confessions of St. Augustine."

These, however, though describing a like spiritual conflict, are couched in a more cultured style, and rise to a higher metaphysical region than Bunyan was capable of attaining to. His level is a lower one, but on that level Bunyan is without a rival. Never has the history of a soul convinced of the reality of eternal perdition in its most terrible form as the most certain of all possible facts, and of its own imminent danger of hopeless, irreversible doom—seeing itself, to employ his own image, hanging, as it were, over the pit of hell by a thin line, which might snap any moment—been portrayed in more nervous and awe-inspiring language.

And its awfulness is enhanced by its self-evident truth. Bunyan was drawing no imaginary picture of what others might feel, but simply telling in plain unadorned language what he had felt. The experience was a very tremendous reality to him. Like Dante, if he had not actually been in hell, he had been on the very threshold of it; he had in very deed traversed "the Valley of the Shadow of Death," had heard its "hideous noises," and seen "the Hobgoblins of the Pit." He "spake what he knew and testified what he had seen." Every sentence breathes the most tremendous earnestness. His words are the plainest, drawn from his own homely vernacular. He says in his preface, which will amply repay reading, as one of the most characteristic specimens of his style, that he could have stepped into a higher style, and adorned his narrative more plentifully.

But he dared not. "God did not play in convincing him. The devil did not play in tempting him. He himself did not play when he sunk as into a bottomless pit, and the pangs of hell caught hold on him. Nor could he play in relating them. He must be plain and simple and lay down the thing as it was. He that liked it might receive it. He that did not might produce a better." The remembrance of "his great sins, his great temptations, his great fears of perishing for ever, recalled the remembrance of his great help, his great support from heaven, the great grace God extended to such a wretch as he was." Having thus enlarged on his own experience, he calls on his spiritual children, for whose use the work was originally composed and to whom it is dedicated,—"those whom God had counted him worthy to beget to Faith by his ministry in the Word"—to survey their own religious history, to "work diligently and leave no corner unsearched."

He would have them "remember their tears and prayers to God; how they sighed under every hedge for mercy. Had they never a hill Mizar (Psa. 42:6) to remember? Had they forgotten the close, the milkhouse, the stable, the barn, where God visited their souls? Let them remember the Word on which the Lord had caused them to hope. If they had sinned against light, if they were tempted to blaspheme, if they were down in despair, let them remember that it had been so with him, their spiritual father, and that out of them all the Lord had delivered him." This dedication ends thus: "My dear children, the milk and honey is beyond this wilderness. God be merciful to you, and grant you be not slothful to go in to possess the land."

This remarkable book, as we learn from the title-page, was "written by his own hand in prison." It was first published by George Larkin in London, in 1666, the sixth year of his imprisonment, the year of the Fire of London, about the time that he experienced his first brief release. As with "The Pilgrim's Progress," the work grew in picturesque detail and graphic power in the author's hand after its first appearance. The later editions supply some of the most interesting personal facts contained in the narrative, which were wanting when it first issued from the press. His two escapes from drowning, and from the supposed sting of an adder; his being drawn as a soldier, and his providential deliverance from death; the graphic account of his difficulty in giving up bell-ringing at Elstow Church, and dancing on Sundays on Elstow Green—these and other minor touches which give a life and colour to the story, which we should be very sorry to lose, are later additions.

It is impossible to over-estimate the value of the "Grace Abounding," both for the facts of Bunyan's earlier life and for the spiritual experience of which these facts were, in his eyes only the outward framework. Beginning with his parentage and boyhood, it carries us down to his marriage and life in the wayside-cottage at Elstow, his introduction to Mr. Gifford's congregation at Bedford, his joining that holy brotherhood, and his subsequent call to the work of the ministry among them, and winds up with an account of his apprehension, examinations, and imprisonment in Bedford gaol.

The work concludes with a report of the conversation between his noble-hearted wife and Sir Matthew Hale and the other judges at the Midsummer assizes, narrated in a former chapter, "taken down," he says, "from her own mouth." The whole story is of such sustained interest that our chief regret on finishing it is that it stops where it does, and does not go on much further. Its importance for our knowledge of Bunyan as a man, as distinguished from an author, and of the circumstances of his life, is seen by a comparison of our acquaintance with his earlier and with his later years. When he laid down his pen no one took it up, and beyond two or three facts, and a few hazy anecdotes we know little or nothing of all that happened between his final release and his death.

The value of the "Grace Abounding," however, as a work of experimental religion may be easily over-estimated. It is not many who can study Bunyan's minute history of the various stages of his spiritual life with real profit. To some temperaments, especially among the young, the book is more likely to prove injurious than beneficial; it is calculated rather to nourish morbid imaginations, and a dangerous habit of introspection, than to foster the quiet growth of the inner life. Bunyan's unhappy mode of dealing with the Bible as a collection of texts, each of Divine authority and declaring a definite meaning entirely irrespective of its context, by which the words hide the Word, is also utterly destructive of the true purpose of the Holy Scriptures as a revelation of God's loving and holy mind and will.

Few things are more touching than the eagerness with which, in his intense self-torture, Bunyan tried to evade the force of those "fearful and terrible Scriptures" which appeared to seal his condemnation, and to lay hold of the promises to the penitent sinner. His tempest-tossed spirit could only find rest by doing violence to the dogma, then universally accepted and not quite extinct even in our own days, that the authority of the Bible—that "Divine Library"—collectively taken, belongs to each and every sentence of the Bible taken for and by itself, and that, in Coleridge's words, "detached sentences from books composed at the distance of centuries, nay, sometimes at a millenium from each other, under different dispensations and for different objects," are to be brought together "into logical dependency."

But "where the Spirit of the Lord is there is liberty." The divinely given life in the soul of man snaps the bonds of humanly-constructed logical systems. Only those, however, who have known by experience the force of Bunyan's spiritual combat, can fully appreciate and profit by Bunyan's narrative. He tells us on the title-page that it was written "for the support of the weak and tempted people of God." For such the "Grace Abounding to the chief of sinners" will ever prove most valuable. Those for whom it was intended will find in it a message—of comfort and strength.

As has been said, Bunyan's pen was almost idle during the last six years of his imprisonment. Only two of his works were produced in this period: his "Confession of Faith," and his "Defence of the Doctrine of Justification by Faith." Both were written very near the end of his prison life, and published in the same year, 1672, only a week or two before his release. The object of the former work was, as Dr. Brown tells us, "to vindicate his teaching, and if possible, to secure his liberty."

Writing as one "in bonds for the Gospel," his professed principles, he asserts, are "faith, and holiness springing therefrom, with an endeavour so far as in him lies to be at peace with all men." He is ready to hold communion with all whose principles are the same; with all whom he can reckon as children of God. With these he will not quarrel about "things that are circumstantial," such as water baptism, which he regards as something quite indifferent, men being "neither the better for having it, nor the worse for having it not." "He will receive them in the Lord as becometh saints. If they will not have communion with him, the neglect is theirs not his.

But with the openly profane and ungodly, though, poor people! they have been christened and take the communion, he will have no communion. It would be a strange community, he says, that consisted of men and beasts. Men do not receive their horse or their dog to their table; they put them in a room by themselves." As regards forms and ceremonies, he "cannot allow his soul to be governed in its approach to God by the superstitious inventions of this world.

He is content to stay in prison even till the moss grows on his eyelids rather than thus make of his conscience a continual butchery and slaughter-shop by putting out his eyes and committing himself to the blind to lead him. Eleven years' imprisonment was a weighty argument to pause and pause again over the foundation of the principles for which he had thus suffered. Those principles he had asserted at his trial, and in the tedious tract of time since then he had in cold blood examined them by the Word of God and found them good; nor could he dare to revolt from or deny them on pain of eternal damnation."

The second-named work, the "Defence of the Doctrine of Justification by Faith," is entirely controversial. The Rev. Edward Fowler, afterwards Bishop of Gloucester, then Rector of Northill, had published in the early part of 1671, a book entitled "The Design of Christianity." A copy having found its way into Bunyan's hands, he was so deeply stirred by what he deemed its subversion of the true foundation of Evangelical religion that he took up his pen and in the space of six weeks composed a long and elaborate examination of the book, chapter by chapter, and a confutation of its teaching.

Fowler's doctrines as Bunyan understood them—or rather misunderstood them—awoke the worst side of his impetuous nature. His vituperation of the author and his book is coarse and unmeasured. He roundly charges Fowler with having "closely, privily, and devilishly turned the grace of God into a licentious doctrine, bespattering it with giving liberty to lasciviousness;" and he calls him "a pretended minister of the Word," who, in "his cursed blasphemous book vilely exposes to public view the rottenness of his heart, in principle diametrically opposite to the simplicity of the Gospel of Christ, a glorious latitudinarian that can, as to religion, turn and twist like an eel on the angle, or rather like the weathercock that stands on the steeple;" and describes him as "contradicting the wholesome doctrine of the Church of England."

He "knows him not by face much less his personal practise." He may have "kept himself clear of the ignorant Sir Johns who had for a long time, as a judgment of God, been made the mouth to the people—men of debauched lives who for the love of filthy lucre and the pampering of their idle carcases had made shipwreck of their former faith;" but he does know that having been ejected as a Nonconformist in 1662, he had afterwards gone over to the winning side, and he fears that "such an unstable weathercock spirit as he had manifested would stumble the work and give advantage to the adversary to speak vilifyingly of religion." No excuse can be offered for the coarse violence of Bunyan's language in this book; but it was too much the habit of the time to load a theological opponent with vituperation, to push his assertions to the furthest extreme, and make the most unwarrantable deductions from them.

It must be acknowledged that Bunyan does not treat Fowler and his doctrines with fairness, and that, if the latter may be thought to depreciate unduly the sacrifice of the Death of Christ as an expiation for man's guilt, and to lay too great a stress on the moral faculties remaining in the soul after the Fall, Bunyan errs still more widely on the other side in asserting the absolute, irredeemable corruption of human nature, leaving nothing for grace to work upon, but demanding an absolutely fresh creation, not a revivification of the Divine nature grievously marred but not annihilated by Adam's sin.

A reply to Bunyan's severe strictures was not slow to appear. The book bears the title, characteristic of the tone and language of its contents, of "Dirt wip't off; or, a manifest discovery of the Gross Ignorance, Erroneousness, and most Unchristian and Wicked Spirit of one John

Bunyan, Lay-preacher in Bedford." It professes to be written by a friend of Fowler's, but Fowler was generally accredited with it. Its violent tirades against one who, he says, had been "near these twenty years or longer very infamous in the Town and County of Bedford as a very Pestilent Schismatick," and whom he suggests the authorities have done wrong in letting out of prison, and had better clap in gaol again as "an impudent and malicious Firebrand," have long since been consigned to a merciful oblivion, where we may safely leave them.

Chapter 8

Bunyan's protracted imprisonment came to an end in 1672. The exact date of his actual liberation is uncertain. His pardon under the Great Seal bears date September 13th. But we find from the church books that he had been appointed pastor of the congregation to which he belonged as early as the 21st of January of that year, and on the 9th of May his ministerial position was duly recognized by the Government, and a license was granted to him to act "as preacher in the house of Josias Roughead," for those "of the Persuasion commonly called Congregational." His release would therefore seem to have anticipated the formal issue of his pardon by four months.

Bunyan was now half way through his forty-fourth year. Sixteen years still remained to him before his career of indefatigable service in the Master's work was brought to a close. Of these sixteen years, as has already been remarked, we have only a very general knowledge. Details are entirely wanting; nor is there any known source from which they can be recovered. If he kept any diary it has not been preserved. If he wrote letters—and one who was looked up to by so large a circle of disciples as a spiritual father and guide, and whose pen was so ready of exercise, cannot fail to have written many—not one has come down to us.

The pages of the church books during his pastorate are also provokingly barren of record, and little that they contain is in Bunyan's handwriting. As Dr. Brown has said, "he seems to have been too busy to keep any records of his busy life." Nor can we fill up the blank from external authorities. The references to Bunyan in contemporary biographies are far fewer than we might have expected; certainly far fewer than we could have desired. But the little that is recorded is eminently characteristic.

We see him constantly engaged in the great work to which he felt God had called him, and for which, "with much content through grace," he had suffered twelve years' incarceration.

In addition to the regular discharge of his pastoral duties to his own congregation, he took a general oversight of the villages far and near which had been the scene of his earlier ministry, preaching whenever opportunity offered, and, ever unsparing of his own personal labour, making long journeys into distant parts of the country for the furtherance of the gospel. We find him preaching at Leicester in the year of his release. Reading also is mentioned as receiving occasional visits from him, and that not without peril after the revival of persecution; while the congregations in London had the benefit of his exhortations at stated intervals.

Almost the first thing Bunyan did, after his liberation from gaol, was to make others sharers in his hardly won "liberty of prophesying," by applying to the Government for licenses for preachers and preaching places in Bedfordshire and the neighbouring counties, under the Declaration of Indulgence. The still existing list sent in to the authorities by him, in his own handwriting, contains the names of twenty-five preachers and thirty buildings, besides "Josias Roughead's House in his orchard at Bedford." Nineteen of these were in his own native county, three in Northamptonshire, three in Buckinghamshire, two in Cambridgeshire, two in Huntingdonshire, and one in Hertfordshire.

The places sought to be licensed were very various, barns, malthouses, halls belonging to public companies, &c., but more usually private houses. Over these religious communities, bound together by a common faith and common suffering, Bunyan exercised a quasi-episcopal superintendence, which gained for him the playful title of "Bishop Bunyan." In his regular circuits,—"visitations" we may not improperly term them,—we are told that he exerted himself to relieve the temporal wants of the sufferers under the penal laws,—so soon and so cruelly revived,—ministered diligently to the sick and afflicted, and used his influence in reconciling differences between "professors of the gospel," and thus prevented the scandal of litigation among Christians.

The closing period of Bunyan's life was laborious but happy, spent "honourably and innocently" in writing, preaching, visiting his congregations, and planting daughter churches. "Happy," writes Mr. Froude, "in his work; happy in the sense that his influence was daily extending—spreading over his own country and to the far-off settlements of America,—he spent his last years in his own land of Beulah, Doubting Castle out of sight, and the towers and minarets of Immanuel's Land growing nearer and clearer as the days went on."

With his time so largely occupied in his spiritual functions, he could have had but small leisure to devote to his worldly calling. This, however, one of so honest and independent a spirit is sure not to have neglected, it was indeed necessary that to a certain extent he should work for his living. He had a family to maintain. His congregation were mostly of the poorer sort, unable to contribute much to their pastor's support. Had it been otherwise, Bunyan was the last man in the world to make a trade of the gospel, and though never hesitating to avail himself of the apostolic privilege to "live of the gospel," he, like the apostle of the Gentiles, would never be ashamed to "work with his own hands," that he might "minister to his own necessities," and those of his family.

But from the time of his release he regarded his ministerial work as the chief work of his life. "When he came abroad," says one who knew him, "he found his temporal affairs were gone to wreck, and he had as to them to begin again as if he had newly come into the world. But yet he was not destitute of friends, who had all along supported him with necessaries and had been very good to his family, so that by their assistance getting things a little about him again, he resolved as much as possible to decline worldly business, and give himself wholly up to the service of God."

The anonymous writer to whom we are indebted for information concerning his imprisonment and his subsequent life, says that Bunyan, "contenting himself with that little God had bestowed upon him, sequestered himself from all secular employments to follow that of his call to the ministry." The fact, however, that in the "deed of gift" of all his property to his wife in 1685, he still describes himself as a "brazier," puts it beyond all doubt that though his ministerial duties were his chief concern, he prudently kept fast hold of his handicraft as a certain means of support for himself and those dependent on him.

On the whole, Bunyan's outward circumstances were probably easy. His wants were few and easily supplied. "Having food and raiment" for himself, his wife, and his children, he was "therewith content." The house in the parish of St. Cuthbert's which was his home from his release to his death (unhappily demolished fifty years back), shows the humble character of his daily life. It was a small cottage, such as labourers now occupy, with three small rooms on the ground floor, and a garret with a diminutive dormer window under the high-pitched tiled roof. Behind stood an outbuilding which served as his workshop.

We have a passing glimpse of this cottage home in the diary of Thomas Hearne, the Oxford antiquary. One Mr. Bagford, otherwise unknown to us, had once "walked into the country" on purpose to see "the study of John Bunyan," and the student who made it famous. On his arrival the interviewer—as we should now call him—met with a civil and courteous reception from Bunyan; but he found the contents of his study hardly larger than those of his prison cell. They were limited to a Bible, and copies of "The Pilgrim's Progress," and a few other books, chiefly his own works, "all lying on a shelf or shelves." Slight as this sketch is, it puts us more in touch with the immortal dreamer than many longer and more elaborate paragraphs.

Bunyan's celebrity as a preacher, great before he was shut up in gaol, was naturally enhanced by the circumstance of his imprisonment. The barn in Josias Roughead's orchard, where he was licensed as a preacher, was "so thronged the first time he appeared there to edify, that many were constrained to stay without; every one that was of his persuasion striving to partake of his instructions."

Wherever he ministered, sometimes, when troublous days returned, in woods, and in dells, and other hiding-places, the announcement that John Bunyan was to preach gathered a large and attentive auditory, hanging on his lips and drinking from them the word of life. His fame grew the more he was known and reached its climax when his work was nearest its end. His biographer Charles Doe tells us that just before his death, "when Mr. Bunyan preached in London, if there were but one day's notice given, there would be more people come together than the meeting-house could hold. I have seen, by my computation, about twelve hundred at a morning lecture by seven o'clock on a working day, in the dark winter time. I also computed about three thousand that came to hear him one Lord's Day in London, at a town's-end meeting-house, so that half were fain to go back again for want of room, and then himself was fain at a back door to be pulled almost over people to get upstairs to his pulpit."

This "town's-end meeting house" has been identified by some with a quaint straggling long building which once stood in Queen Street, Southwark, of which there is an engraving in Wilkinson's "Londina Illustrata." Doe's account, however, probably points to another building, as the Zoar Street meeting-house was not opened for worship till about six months before Bunyan's death, and then for Presbyterian service. Other places in London connected with his preaching are Pinners' Hall in Old Broad Street, where, on one of his occasional visits, he delivered his striking sermon on "The Greatness of the Soul and the Unspeakableness of the Loss thereof," first published in 1683; and Dr. Owen's meeting-house in White's Alley, Moorfields, which was the gathering-place for titled folk, city merchants, and other Nonconformists of position and degree.

At earlier times, when the penal laws against Nonconformists were in vigorous exercise, Bunyan had to hold his meetings by stealth in private houses and other places where he might hope to escape the lynx-eyed informer. It was at one of these furtive meetings that his earliest biographer, the honest combmaker at the foot of London Bridge,

Charles Doe, first heard him preach. His choice of an Old Testament text at first offended Doe, who had lately come into New Testament light and had had enough of the "historical and doing-for-favour of the Old Testament." But as he went on he preached "so New Testament like" that his hearer's prejudices vanished, and he could only "admire, weep for joy, and give the preacher his affections."

Bunyan was more than once urged to leave Bedford and settle in the metropolis. But to all these solicitations he turned a deaf ear. Bedford was the home of his deepest affections. It was there the holy words of the poor women "sitting in the sun," speaking "as if joy did make them speak," had first "made his heart shake," and shown him that he was still a stranger to vital godliness. It was there he had been brought out of darkness into light himself, and there too he had been the means of imparting the same blessing to others. The very fact of his long imprisonment had identified him with the town and its inhabitants. There he had a large and loving congregation, to whom he was bound by the ties of a common faith and common sufferings.

Many of these recognized in Bunyan their spiritual father; all, save a few "of the baser sort," reverenced him as their teacher and guide. No prospect of a wider field of usefulness, still less of a larger income, could tempt him to desert his "few sheep in the wilderness." Some of them, it is true, were wayward sheep, who wounded the heart of their pastor by breaking from the fold, and displaying very un-lamb-like behaviour. He had sometimes to realize painfully that no pale is so close but that the enemy will creep in somewhere and seduce the flock; and that no rules of communion, however strict, can effectually exclude unworthy members. Brother John Stanton had to be admonished "for abusing his wife and beating her often for very light matters" (if the matters had been less light, would the beating in these days have been thought justifiable?); and Sister Mary Foskett, for "privately whispering of a horrid scandal, 'without culler of truth,' against Brother Honeylove."

Evil-speaking and backbiting set brother against brother. Dissensions and heartburnings grieved Bunyan's spirit. He himself was not always spared. A letter had to be written to Sister Hawthorn "by way of reproof for her unseemly language against Brother Scot and the whole Church." John Wildman was had up before the Church and convicted of being "an abominable liar and slanderer," "extraordinary guilty" against "our beloved Brother Bunyan himself." And though Sister Hawthorn satisfied the Church by "humble acknowledgment of her miscariag," the bolder misdoer only made matters worse by "a frothy letter," which left no alternative but a sentence of expulsion.

But though Bunyan's flock contained some whose fleeces were not as white as he desired, these were the exception. The congregation meeting in Josias Roughead's barn must have been, take them as a whole, a quiet, God-fearing, spiritually-minded folk, of whom their pastor could think with thankfulness and satisfaction as "his hope and joy and crown of rejoicing." From such he could not be severed lightly. Inducements which would have been powerful to a meaner nature fell dead on his independent spirit. He was not "a man that preached by way of bargain for money," and, writes Doe, "more than once he refused a more plentiful income to keep his station." As Dr. Brown says: "He was too deeply rooted on the scene of his lifelong labours and sufferings to think of striking his tent till the command came from the Master to come up to the higher service for which he had been ripening so long."

At Bedford, therefore, he remained; quietly staying on in his cottage in St. Cuthbert's, and ministering to his humble flock, loving and beloved, as Mr. Froude writes, "through changes of ministry, Popish plots, and Monmouth rebellions, while the terror of a restoration of Popery was bringing on the Revolution; careless of kings and cabinets, and confident that Giant Pope had lost his power for harm, and thenceforward could only bite his nails at the passing pilgrims."

Bunyan's peace was not, however, altogether undisturbed. Once it received a shock in a renewal of his imprisonment, though only for a brief period, in 1675, to which we owe the world-famous "Pilgrim's Progress"; and it was again threatened, though not actually disturbed ten years later, when the renewal of the persecution of the Nonconformists induced him to make over all his property—little enough in good sooth—to his wife by deed of gift.

The former of these events demands our attention, not so much for itself as for its connection with Bishop Barlow's interference in Bunyan's behalf, and, still more, for its results in the production of "The Pilgrim's Progress." Until very recently the bare fact of this later imprisonment, briefly mentioned by Charles Doe and another of his early biographers, was all that was known to us. They even leave the date to be gathered, though both agree in limiting its duration to six months or thereabouts.

The recent discovery, among the Chauncey papers, by Mr. W. G. Thorpe, of the original warrant under which Bunyan was at this time sent to gaol, supplies the missing information. It has been already noticed that the Declaration of Indulgence, under which Bunyan was liberated in 1672, was very short lived. Indeed it barely lasted in force a twelvemonth. Granted on the 15th of March of that year, it was withdrawn on the 9th of March of the following year, at the instance of the House of Commons, who had taken alarm at a suspension of the laws of the realm by the "inherent power" of the sovereign, without the advice or sanction of Parliament.

The Declaration was cancelled by Charles II., the monarch, it is said, tearing off the Great Seal with his own hands, a subsidy being promised to the royal spendthrift as a reward for his complaisance. The same year the Test Act became law. Bunyan therefore and his fellow Nonconformists were in a position of greater peril, as far as the letter of the law was concerned, than they had ever been. But, as Dr. Stoughton has remarked, "the letter of the law is not to be taken as an accurate index of the Nonconformists' condition. The pressure of a bad law depends very much upon the hands employed in its administration." Unhappily for Bunyan, the parties in whose hands the execution of the penal statutes against Nonconformists rested in Bedfordshire were his bitter personal enemies, who were not likely to let them lie inactive.

The prime mover in the matter was doubtless Dr. William Foster, that "right Judas" whom we shall remember holding the candle in Bunyan's face in the hall of Harlington House at his first apprehension, and showing such feigned affection "as if he would have leaped on his neck and kissed him." He had some time before this become Chancellor of the Bishop of Lincoln, and Commissary of the Court of the Archdeacon of Bedford, offices which put in his hands extensive powers which he had used with the most relentless severity. He has damned himself to eternal infamy by the bitter zeal he showed in hunting down Dissenters, inflicting exorbitant fines, and breaking into their houses and distraining their goods for a full discharge, maltreating their wives and daughters, and haling the offenders to prison.

Having been chiefly instrumental in Bunyan's first committal to gaol, he doubtless viewed his release with indignation as the leader of the Bedfordshire sectaries who was doing more mischief to the cause of conformity, which it was his province at all hazards to maintain, than any other twenty men. The church would never be safe till he was clapped in prison again. The power to do this was given by the new proclamation. By this act the licenses to preach previously granted to Nonconformists were recalled. Henceforward no conventicle had "any authority, allowance, or encouragement from his Majesty." We can easily imagine the delight with which Foster would hail the issue of this proclamation. How he would read and read again with ever fresh satisfaction its stringent clauses. That pestilent fellow, Bunyan, was now once more in his clutches. This time there was no chance of his escape.

All licences were recalled, and he was absolutely defenceless. It should not be Foster's fault if he failed to end his days in the prison from which he ought never to have been released. The proclamation is dated the 4th of March, 1674-5, and was published in the Gazette on the 9th. It would reach Bedford on the 11th. It placed Bunyan at the mercy of "his enemies, who struck at him forthwith." A warrant was issued for his apprehension, undoubtedly written by our old friend, Paul Cobb, the clerk of the peace, who, it will be remembered, had acted in the same capacity on Bunyan's first committal. It is dated the 4th of March, and bears the signature of no fewer than thirteen magistrates, ten of them affixing their seals.

That so unusually large a number took part in the execution of this warrant, is sufficient indication of the importance attached to Bunyan's imprisonment by the gentry of the county. The following is the document:—

To the Constables of Bedford and to every of them

Whereas information and complaint is made unto us that (notwithstanding the Kings Majesties late Act of most gracious general and free pardon to all his subjects for past misdemeanours that by his said clemency and indulgent grace and favor they might be moved and induced for the time to come more carefully to observe his Highness law and Statutes and to continue in their loyal and due obedience to his Majesty) Yet one John Bunyon of your said Towne Tynker hath divers times within one month last past in contempt of his Majesty's good Laws preached or teached at a Conventicle Meeting or Assembly under color or pretence of exercise of Religion in other manner than according to the Liturgie or practice of the Church of England These are therefore in his Majesty's name to comand you forthwith to apprehend and bring the Body of the said John Bunnion before us or any of us or other his Majesty's Justice of Peace within the said County to answer the premises and further to do and receive as to Law and Justice shall appertaine and hereof you are not to fail. Given under our hands and seals this fourth day of March in the seven and twentieth year of the Reign of our most gracious Sovereign Lord King Charles the Second, 1674.

J Napier, W Beecher, G Blundell, Hum Monoux, Will Franklin, John Ventris, Will Spencer, Will Gery, St Jo Chernocke, Wm Daniels, T Browne, W Foster, Gaius Squire.

There would be little delay in the execution of the warrant.

John Bunyan was a marked man and an old offender, who, on his arrest, would be immediately committed for trial. Once more, then, Bunyan became a prisoner, and that, there can be little doubt, in his old quarters in the Bedford gaol. Errors die hard, and those by whom they have been once accepted find it difficult to give them up. The long-standing tradition of Bunyan's twelve years' imprisonment in the little lock-up-house on the Ouse bridge, having been scattered to the winds by the logic of fact and common sense, those to whom the story is dear, including the latest and ablest of his biographers, Dr. Brown, see in this second brief imprisonment a way to rehabilitate it.

Probability pointing to this imprisonment as the time of the composition of "The Pilgrim's Progress," they hold that on this occasion Bunyan was committed to the bridge-gaol, and that he there wrote his immortal work, though they fail to bring forward any satisfactory reasons for the change of the place of his confinement. The circumstances, however, being the same, there can be no reasonable ground for questioning that, as before, Bunyan was imprisoned in the county gaol.

This last imprisonment of Bunyan's lasted only half as many months as his former imprisonment had lasted years. At the end of six months he was again a free man. His release was due to the good officers of Owen, Cromwell's celebrated chaplain, with Barlow, Bishop of Lincoln. The suspicion which hung over this intervention from its being erroneously attributed to his release in 1672, three years before Barlow became a bishop, has been dispelled by the recently discovered warrant. The dates and circumstances are now found to tally.

The warrant for Bunyan's apprehension bears date March 4, 1675. On the 14th of the following May the supple and time-serving Barlow, after long and eager waiting for a mitre, was elected to the see of Lincoln vacated by the death of Bishop Fuller, and consecrated on the 27th of June. Barlow, a man of very dubious churchmanship, who had succeeded in keeping his university appointments undisturbed all through the Commonwealth, and who was yet among the first with effusive loyalty to welcome the restoration of monarchy, had been Owen's tutor at Oxford, and continued to maintain friendly relations with him. As bishop of the diocese to which Bedfordshire then, and long after, belonged, Barlow had the power, by the then existing law, of releasing a prisoner for nonconformity on a bond given by two persons that he would conform within half a year.

A friend of Bunyan's, probably Ichabod Chauncey, obtained a letter from Owen to the bishop requesting him to employ this prerogative in Bunyan's behalf. Barlow with hollow complaisance expressed his particular kindness for Dr. Owen, and his desire to deny him nothing he could legally grant. He would even strain a point to serve him. But he had only just been made a bishop, and what was asked was a new thing to him. He desired a little time to consider of it. If he could do it, Owen might be assured of his readiness to oblige him. A second application at the end of a fortnight found this readiness much cooled. It was true that on inquiry he found he might do it; but the times were critical, and he had many enemies. It would be safer for him not to take the initiative. Let them apply to the Lord Chancellor, and get him to issue an order for him to release Bunyan on the customary bond. Then he would do what Owen asked.

It was vain to tell Barlow that the way he suggested was chargeable, and Bunyan poor. Vain also to remind him that there was no point to be strained. He had satisfied himself that he might do the thing legally. It was hoped he would remember his promise. But the bishop would not budge from the position he had taken up. They had his ultimatum; with that they must be content. If Bunyan was to be liberated, his friends must accept Barlow's terms. "This at last was done, and the poor man was released. But little thanks to the bishop."

This short six months' imprisonment assumes additional importance from the probability, first suggested by Dr. Brown, which the recovery of its date renders almost a certainty, that it was during this period that Bunyan began, if he did not complete, the first part of "The Pilgrim's Progress." We know from Bunyan's own words that the book was begun in gaol, and its composition has been hitherto unhesitatingly assigned to his twelve years' confinement. Dr. Brown was, we believe, the first to call this in question. Bunyan's imprisonment, we know, ended in 1672.

The first edition of "The Pilgrim's Progress" did not appear till 1678. If written during his earlier imprisonment, six years must have elapsed between its writing and its publication. But it was not Bunyan's way to keep his works in manuscript so long after their completion. His books were commonly put in the printers' hands as soon as they were finished. There are no sufficient reasons—though some have been suggested—for his making an exception to this general habit in the case of "The Pilgrim's Progress." Besides we should certainly conclude, from the poetical introduction, that there was little delay between the finishing of the book and its being given to the world. After having written the book, he tells us, simply to gratify himself, spending only "vacant seasons" in his "scribble," to "divert" himself "from worser thoughts," he showed it to his friends to get their opinion whether it should be published or not. But as they were not all of one mind, but some counselled one thing and some another, after some perplexity, he took the matter into his own hands.

> Now was I in a strait, and did not see
> Which was the best thing to be done by me;
> At last I thought, Since you are so divided,
> I print it will, and so the case decided.

We must agree with Dr. Brown that "there is a briskness about this which, to say the least, is not suggestive of a six years' interval before publication." The break which occurs in the narrative after the visit of the Pilgrims to the Delectable Mountains, which so unnecessarily interrupts the course of the story—"So I awoke from my dream; and I slept and dreamed again"—has been not unreasonably thought by Dr. Brown to indicate the point Bunyan had reached when his six months' imprisonment ended, and from which he continued the book after his release.

The First Part of "The Pilgrim's Progress" issued from the press in 1678. A second edition followed in the same year, and a third with large and important additions in 1679. The Second Part, after an interval of seven years, followed early in 1685. Between the two parts appeared two of his most celebrated works—the "Life and Death of Mr. Badman," published in 1680, originally intended to supply a contrast and a foil to "The Pilgrim's Progress," by depicting a life which was scandalously bad; and, in 1682, that which Macaulay, with perhaps exaggerated eulogy, has said, "would have been our greatest allegory if the earlier allegory had never been written," the "Holy War made by Shaddai upon Diabolus." Superior to "The Pilgrim's Progress" as a literary composition, this last work must be pronounced decidedly inferior to it in attractive power. For one who reads the "Holy War," five hundred read the "Pilgrim."

And those who read it once return to it again and again, with ever fresh delight. It is a book that never tires. One or two perusals of the "Holy War" satisfy: and even these are not without weariness. As Mr. Froude has said, "The 'Holy War' would have entitled Bunyan to a place among the masters of English literature. It would never have made his name a household word in every English-speaking family on the globe."

Leaving the further notice of these and his other chief literary productions to another chapter, there is little more to record in Bunyan's life. Though never again seriously troubled for his nonconformity, his preaching journeys were not always without risk. There is a tradition that when he visited Reading to preach, he disguised himself as a waggoner carrying a long whip in his hand to escape detection. The name of "Bunyan's Dell," in a wood not very far from Hitchin, tells of the time when he and his hearers had to conceal their meetings from their enemies' quest, with scouts planted on every side to warn them of the approach of the spies and informers, who for reward were actively plying their odious trade. Reference has already been made to Bunyan's "deed of gift" of all that he possessed in the world—his "goods, chattels, debts, ready money, plate, rings, household stuff, apparel, utensils, brass, pewter, bedding, and all other his substance whatsoever—to his well-beloved wife Elizabeth Bunyan."

owards the close of the first year of James the Second, 1685, the apprehensions under which Bunyan executed this document were far from groundless. At no time did the persecution of Nonconformists rage with greater fierceness. Never, not even under the tyranny of Laud, as Lord Macaulay records had the condition of the Puritans been so deplorable. Never had spies been so actively employed in detecting congregations. Never had magistrates, grand-jurors, rectors, and church-wardens been so much on the alert. Many Nonconformists were cited before the ecclesiastical courts. Others found it necessary to purchase the connivance of the agents of the Government by bribes. It was impossible for the sectaries to pray together without precautions such as are employed by coiners and receivers of stolen goods.

Dissenting ministers, however blameless in life, however eminent in learning, could not venture to walk the streets for fear of outrages which were not only not repressed, but encouraged by those whose duty it was to preserve the peace. Richard Baxter was in prison. Howe was afraid to show himself in London for fear of insult, and had been driven to Utrecht. Not a few who up to that time had borne up boldly lost heart and fled the kingdom. Other weaker spirits were terrified into a show of conformity. Through many subsequent years the autumn of 1685 was remembered as a time of misery and terror.

There is, however, no indication of Bunyan having been molested. The "deed of gift" by which he sought to avoid the confiscation of his goods was never called into exercise. Indeed its very existence was forgotten by his wife in whose behalf it had been executed. Hidden away in a recess in his house in St. Cuthbert's, this interesting document was accidentally discovered at the beginning of the present century, and is preserved among the most valued treasures of the congregation which bears his name.

Quieter times for Nonconformists were however at hand. Active persecution was soon to cease for them, and happily never to be renewed in England. The autumn of 1685 showed the first indications of a great turn of fortune, and before eighteen months had elapsed, the intolerant king and the intolerant Church were eagerly bidding against each other for the support of the party which both had so deeply injured. A new form of trial now awaited the Nonconformists. Peril to their personal liberty was succeeded by a still greater peril to their honesty and consistency of spirit. James the Second, despairing of employing the Tories and the Churchmen as his tools, turned, as his brother had turned before him, to the Dissenters.

The snare was craftily baited with a Declaration of Indulgence, by which the king, by his sole authority, annulled a long series of statutes and suspended all penal laws against Nonconformists of every sort. These lately political Pariahs now held the balance of power. The future fortunes of England depended mainly on the course they would adopt. James was resolved to convert the House of Commons from a free deliberative assembly into a body subservient to his wishes, and ready to give parliamentary sanction to any edict he might issue. To obtain this end the electors must be manipulated. Leaving the county constituencies to be dealt with by the lords-lieutenants, half of whom preferred dismissal to carrying out the odious service peremptorily demanded of them, James's next concern was to "regulate" the Corporations.

In those days of narrowly restricted franchise, the municipalities virtually returned the town members. To obtain an obedient parliament, he must secure a roll of electors pledged to return the royal nominees. A committee of seven privy councillors, all Roman Catholics but the infamous Jeffreys, presided over the business, with local sub-committees scattered over the country to carry out the details. Bedford was dealt with in its turn. Under James's policy of courting the Puritans, the leading Dissenters were the first persons to be approached. Two are specially named, a Mr. Margetts, formerly Judge-Advocate-General of the Army under General Monk, and John Bunyan. It is no matter of surprise that

Bunyan, who had been so severe a sufferer under the old penal statutes, should desire their abrogation, and express his readiness to "steer his friends and followers" to support candidates who would pledge themselves to vote for their repeal. But no further would he go.

The Bedford Corporation was "regulated," which means that nearly the whole of its members were removed and others substituted by royal order. Of these new members some six or seven were leading persons of Bunyan's congregation. But, with all his ardent desire for religious liberty, Bunyan was too keen-witted not to see through James's policy, and too honest to give it any direct insidious support. "In vain is the net spread in the sight of any bird." He clearly saw that it was not for any love of the Dissenters that they were so suddenly delivered from their persecutions, and placed on a kind of equality with the Church. The king's object was the establishment of Popery. To this the Church was the chief obstacle. That must be undermined and subverted first. That done, all other religious denominations would follow.

All that the Nonconformists would gain by yielding, was the favour Polyphemus promised Ulysses, to be devoured last. Zealous as he was for the "liberty of prophesying," even that might be purchased at too high a price. The boon offered by the king was "good in itself," but not "so intended." So, as his biographer describes, when the regulators came, "he expressed his zeal with some weariness as perceiving the bad consequences that would ensue, and laboured with his congregation" to prevent their being imposed on by the fair promises of those who were at heart the bitterest enemies of the cause they professed to advocate. The newly-modelled corporation of Bedford seems like the other corporations through the country, to have proved as unmanageable as the old. As Macaulay says, "The sectaries who had declared in favour of the Indulgence had become generally ashamed of their error, and were desirous to make atonement."

Not knowing the man they had to deal with, the "regulators" are said to have endeavoured to buy Bunyan's support by the offer of some place under government. The bribe was indignantly rejected. Bunyan even refused to see the government agent who offered it,—"he would, by no means come to him, but sent his excuse." Behind the treacherous sunshine he saw a black cloud, ready to break. The Ninevites' remedy he felt was now called for. So he gathered his congregation together and appointed a day of fasting and prayer to avert the danger that, under a specious pretext, again menaced their civil and religious liberties. A true, sturdy Englishman, Bunyan, with Baxter and Howe, "refused an indulgence which could only be purchased by the violent overthrow of the law."

Bunyan did not live to see the Revolution. Four months after he had witnessed the delirious joy which hailed the acquittal of the seven bishops, the Pilgrim's earthly Progress ended, and he was bidden to cross the dark river which has no bridge. The summons came to him in the very midst of his religious activity, both as a preacher and as a writer. His pen had never been more busy than when he was bidden to lay it down finally. Early in 1688, after a two years' silence, attributable perhaps to the political troubles of the times, his "Jerusalem Sinner Saved, or a Help to Despairing Souls," one of the best known and most powerfully characteristic of his works, had issued from the press, and had been followed by four others between March and August, the month of his death. These books were, "The Work of Jesus Christ as an Advocate;" a poetical composition entitled "The Building, Nature, and Excellency of the House of God," a discourse on the constitution and government of the Christian Church; the "Water of Life," and "Solomon's Temple Spiritualized." At the time of his death he was occupied in seeing through the press a sixth book, "The Acceptable Sacrifice," which was published after his funeral.

In addition to these, Bunyan left behind him no fewer than fourteen works in manuscript, written at this time, as the fruit of his fertile imagination and untiring pen. Ten of these were given to the world soon after Bunyan's death, by one of Bunyan's most devoted followers, Charles Doe, the combmaker of London Bridge (who naively tells us how one day between the stairhead and the middle of the stairs, he resolved that the best work he could do for God was to get Bunyan's books printed and sell them—adding, "I have sold about 3,000"), and others, a few years later, including one of the raciest of his compositions, "The Heavenly Footman," bought by Doe of Bunyan's eldest son, and, he says, "put into the World in Print Word for Word as it came from him to Me."

At the time that death surprised him, Bunyan had gained no small celebrity in London as a popular preacher, and approached the nearest to a position of worldly honour. Though we must probably reject the idea that he ever filled the office of Chaplain to the Lord Mayor of London, Sir John Shorter, the fact that he is styled "his Lordship's teacher" proves that there was some relation more than that of simple friendship between the chief magistrate and the Bedford minister. But the society of the great was never congenial to him. If they were godly as well as great, he would not shrink from intercourse, with those of a rank above his own, but his heart was with his own humble folk at Bedford. Worldly advancement he rejected for his family as well as for himself. A London merchant, it is said, offered to take his son Joseph into his house of business without the customary premium. But the offer was declined with what we may consider an overstrained independence. "God," he said, "did not send me to advance my family but to preach the gospel." "An instance of other-worldliness," writes Dr. Brown, "perhaps more consistent with the honour of the father than with the prosperity of the son."

Bunyan's end was in keeping with his life. He had ever sought to be a peacemaker and to reconcile differences, and thus had "hindered many mishaps and saved many families from ruin." His last effort of the kind caused his death. The father of a young man in whom he took an interest, had resolved, on some offence, real or supposed, to disinherit his son. The young man sought Bunyan's mediation. Anxious to heal the breach, Bunyan mounted his horse and took the long journey to the father's house at Reading—the scene, as we have noticed, of his occasional ministrations—where he pleaded the offender's cause so effectually as to obtain a promise of forgiveness. Bunyan returned homewards through London, where he was appointed to preach at Mr. Gamman's meeting-house near Whitechapel. His forty miles' ride to London was through heavy driving rain. He was weary and drenched to the skin when he reached the house of his "very loving friend," John Strudwick, grocer and chandler, at the sign of the Star, Holborn Bridge, at the foot of Snow Hill, and deacon of the Nonconformist meeting in Red Cross Street. A few months before Bunyan had suffered from the sweating sickness. The exposure caused a return of the malady, and though well enough to fulfil his pulpit engagement on Sunday, the 19th of August, on the following Tuesday dangerous symptoms declared themselves, and in ten days the disease proved fatal. He died within two months of completing his sixtieth year, on the 31st of August, 1688, just a month before the publication of the Declaration of the Prince of Orange opened a new era of civil and religious liberty, and between two and three months before the Prince's landing in Torbay. He was buried in Mr. Strudwick's newly-purchased vault, in what Southey has termed the Campo Santo of Nonconformists, the burial-ground in Finsbury, taking its name of Bunhill or Bonehill Field, from a vast mass of human remains removed to it from the charnel house of St. Paul's Cathedral in 1549. At a later period it served as a place of interment for those who died in the Great Plague of 1665. The day after Bunyan's funeral, his powerful friend, Sir John Shorter, the Lord Mayor, had a fatal fall from his horse in Smithfield, and "followed him across the river."

By his first wife, whose Christian name is nowhere recorded, Bunyan had four children—two sons and two daughters; and by his second wife, the heroic Elizabeth, one son and one daughter. All of these survived him except his eldest daughter Mary, his tenderly-loved blind child, who died before him. His wife only survived him for a brief period, "following her faithful pilgrim from this world to the other whither he was gone before her" either in 1691 or 1692. Forgetful of the "deed of gift," or ignorant of its bearing, Bunyan's widow took out letters of administration of her late husband's estate, which appears from the Register

Book to have amounted to no more than, £42 19s. On this, and the proceeds of his books, she supported herself till she rejoined him.

Bunyan's character and person are thus described by Charles Doe: "He appeared in countenance to be of a stern and rough temper. But in his conversation he was mild and affable, not given to loquacity or much discourse in company, unless some urgent occasion required it. Observing never to boast of himself or his parts, but rather to seem low in his own eyes and submit himself to the judgment of others. Abhorring lying and swearing, being just, in all that lay in his power, to his word. Not seeming to revenge injuries; loving to reconcile differences and make friendship with all. He had a sharp, quick eye, with an excellent discerning of persons, being of good judgment and quick wit. He was tall of stature, strong-boned, though not corpulent; somewhat of a ruddy face, with sparkling eyes, wearing his hair on his upper lip after the old British fashion. His hair reddish, but in his later days time had sprinkled it with grey. His nose well set, but not declining or bending. His mouth moderately large, his forehead something high, and his habit always plain and modest. Not puffed up in prosperity, nor shaken in adversity, always holding the golden mean."

We may add the portrait drawn by one who had been his companion and fellow-sufferer for many years, John Nelson: "His countenance was grave and sedate, and did so to the life discover the inward frame of his heart, that it was convincing to the beholders and did strike something of awe into them that had nothing of the fear of God."

The same friend speaks thus of Bunyan's preaching: "As a minister of Christ he was laborious in his work of preaching, diligent in his preparation for it, and faithful in dispensing the Word, not sparing reproof whether in the pulpit or no, yet ready to succour the tempted; a son of consolation to the broken-hearted, yet a son of thunder to secure and dead sinners. His memory was tenacious, it being customary with him to commit his sermons to writing after he had preached them. A rich anointing of the Spirit was upon him, yet this great saint was always in his own eyes the chiefest of sinners and the least of saints."

An anecdote is told which, Southey says, "authenticates itself," that one day when he had preached "with peculiar warmth and enlargement," one of his hearers remarked "what a sweet sermon he had delivered." "Ay," was Bunyan's reply, "you have no need to tell me that, for the devil whispered it to me before I was well out of the pulpit." As an evidence of the estimation in which Bunyan was held by the highly-educated, it is recorded that Charles the Second expressed his surprise to Dr. Owen that "a learned man such as he could sit and listen to an illiterate tinker." "May it please your Majesty," Owen replied. "I would gladly give up all my learning if I could preach like that tinker."

Although much of Bunyan's literary activity was devoted to controversy, he had none of the narrowness or bitter spirit of a controversialist. It is true that his zeal for what he deemed to be truth led him into vehemence of language in dealing with those whom he regarded as its perverters. But this intensity of speech was coupled with the utmost charity of spirit towards those who differed from him. Few ever had less of the sectarian temper which lays greater stress on the infinitely small points on which all true Christians differ than on the infinitely great truths on which they are agreed.

Bunyan inherited from his spiritual father, John Gifford, a truly catholic spirit. External differences he regarded as insignificant where he found real Christian faith and love. "I would be," he writes, "as I hope I am, a Christian. But for those factious titles of Anabaptist, Independent, Presbyterian, and the like, I conclude that they come neither from Jerusalem nor from Antioch, but from Hell or from Babylon." "He was," writes one of his early biographers, "a true lover of all that love our Lord Jesus, and did often bewail the different and distinguishing appellations that are among the godly, saying he did believe a time would come when they should be all buried." The only persons he scrupled to hold communion with were those whose lives were openly immoral. "Divisions about non-essentials," he said, "were to churches what wars were to countries.

Those who talked most about religion cared least for it; and controversies about doubtful things and things of little moment, ate up all zeal for things which were practical and indisputable." His last sermon breathed the same catholic spirit, free from the trammels of narrow sectarianism. "If you are the children of God live together lovingly. If the world quarrel with you it is no matter; but it is sad if you quarrel together. If this be among you it is a sign of ill-breeding. Dost thou see a soul that has the image of God in him? Love him, love him. Say, 'This man and I must go to heaven one day.' Serve one another. Do good for one another. If any wrong you pray to God to right you, and love the brotherhood."

The closing words of this his final testimony are such as deserve to be written in letters of gold as the sum of all true Christian teaching: "Be ye holy in all manner of conversation: Consider that the holy God is your Father, and let this oblige you to live like the children of God, that you may look your Father in the face with comfort another day." "There is," writes Dean Stanley, "no compromise in his words, no faltering in his convictions; but his love and admiration are reserved on the whole for that which all good men love, and his detestation on the whole is reserved for that which all good men detest." By the catholic spirit which breathes through his writings, especially through "The Pilgrim's Progress," the tinker of Elstow "has become the teacher not of any particular sect, but of the Universal Church."

Chapter 9

We have, in this concluding chapter, to take a review of Bunyan's merits as a writer, with especial reference to the works on which his fame mainly rests, and, above all, to that which has given him his chief title to be included in a series of Great Writers, "The Pilgrim's Progress." Bunyan, as we have seen, was a very copious author. His works, as collected by the late industrious Mr. Offor, fill three bulky quarto volumes, each of nearly eight hundred double-columned pages in small type.

And this copiousness of production is combined with a general excellence in the matter produced. While few of his books approach the high standard of "The Pilgrim's Progress" or "Holy War," none, it may be truly said, sink very far below that standard. It may indeed be affirmed that it was impossible for Bunyan to write badly. His genius was a native genius. As soon as he began to write at all, he wrote well. Without any training, is he says, in the school of Aristotle or Plato, or any study of the great masters of literature, at one bound he leapt to a high level of thought and composition. His earliest book, "Some Gospel Truths Opened," "thrown off," writes Dr. Brown, "at a heat," displays the same ease of style and directness of speech and absence of stilted phraseology which he maintained to the end.

The great charm which pervades all Bunyan's writings is their naturalness. You never feel that he is writing for effect, still less to perform an uncongenial piece of task-work. He writes because he had something to say which was worth saying, a message to deliver on which the highest interests of others were at stake, which demanded nothing more than a straightforward earnestness and plainness of speech, such as coming from the heart might best reach the hearts of others. He wrote as he spoke, because a necessity was laid upon him which he dared not evade. As he says in a passage quoted in a former chapter, he might have stepped into a much higher style, and have employed more literary ornament. But to attempt this would be, to one of his intense earnestness, to degrade his calling. He dared not do it.

Like the great Apostle, "his speech and preaching was not with enticing words of man's wisdom, but in demonstration of the Spirit and in power." God had not played with him, and he dared not play with others. His errand was much too serious, and their need and danger too urgent to waste time in tricking out his words with human skill. And it is just this which, with all their rudeness, their occasional bad grammar, and homely colloquialisms, gives to Bunyan's writings a power of riveting the attention and stirring the affections which few writers have attained to. The pent-up fire glows in every line, and kindles the hearts of his readers. "Beautiful images, vivid expressions, forcible arguments all aglow with passion, tender pleadings, solemn warnings, make those who read him all eye, all ear, all soul."

This native vigour is attributable, in no small degree, to the manner in which for the most part Bunyan's works came into being. He did not set himself to compose theological treatises upon stated subjects, but after he had preached with satisfaction to himself and acceptance with his audience, he usually wrote out the substance of his discourse from memory, with the enlargements and additions it might seem to require. And thus his religious works have all the glow and fervour of the unwritten utterances of a practised orator, united with the orderliness and precision of a theologian, and are no less admirable for the excellence of their arrangement than for their evangelical spirit and scriptural doctrine. Originally meant to be heard, they lose somewhat by being read. But few can read them without being delighted with the opulence of his imagination and impressed with the solemn earnestness of his convictions. Like the subject of the portrait described by him in the House of the Interpreter, he stands "like one who pleads with men, the law of truth written upon his lips, the world behind his back, and a crown of gold above his head."

These characteristics, which distinguish Bunyan as a writer from most of his Puritan contemporaries, are most conspicuous in the works by which he is chiefly known, "The Pilgrim's Progress," the "Holy War," the "Grace Abounding," and we may add, though from the repulsiveness of the subject the book is now scarcely read at all, the "Life and Death of Mr. Badman."

One great charm of these works, especially of "The Pilgrim's Progress," lies in the pure Saxon English in which they are written, which render them models of the English speech, plain but never vulgar, homely but never coarse, and still less unclean, full of imagery but never obscure, always intelligible, always forcible, going straight to the point in the fewest and simplest words; "powerful and picturesque," writes Hallam, "from concise simplicity." Bunyan's style is recommended by Lord Macaulay as an invaluable study to every person who wishes to gain a wide command over his mother tongue. Its vocabulary is the vocabulary of the common people. "There is not," he truly says, "in 'The Pilgrim's Progress' a single expression, if we except a few technical terms of theology, that would puzzle the rudest peasant."

We may, look through whole pages, and not find a word of more than two syllables. Nor is the source of this pellucid clearness and imaginative power far to seek. Bunyan was essentially a man of one book, and that book the very best, not only for its spiritual teaching but for the purity of its style, the English Bible. "In no book," writes Mr. J. R. Green, "do we see more clearly than in 'The Pilgrim's Progress' the new imaginative force which had been given to the common life of Englishmen by their study of the Bible. Bunyan's English is the simplest and homeliest English that has ever been used by any great English writer, but it is the English of the Bible. His images are the images of prophet and evangelist. So completely had the Bible become Bunyan's life that one feels its phrases as the natural expression of his thoughts. He had lived in the Bible till its words became his own."

All who have undertaken to take an estimate of Bunyan's literary genius call special attention to the richness of his imaginative power. Few writers indeed have possessed this power in so high a degree. In nothing, perhaps, is its vividness more displayed than in the reality of its impersonations. The dramatis persons are not shadowy abstractions, moving far above us in a mystical world, or lay figures ticketed with certain names, but solid men and women of our own flesh and blood, living in our own everyday world, and of like passions with ourselves. Many of them we know familiarly; there is hardly one we should be surprised to meet any day. This lifelike power of characterization belongs in the highest degree to "The Pilgrim's Progress."

It is hardly inferior in "The Holy War," though with some exceptions the people of "Mansoul" have failed to engrave themselves on the popular memory as the characters of the earlier allegory have done. The secret of this graphic power, which gives "The Pilgrim's Progress" its universal popularity, is that Bunyan describes men and women of his own day, such as he had known and seen them. They are not fancy pictures, but literal portraits. Though the features may be exaggerated, and the colours laid on with an unsparing brush, the outlines of his bold personifications are truthfully drawn from his own experience. He had had to do with every one of them. He could have given a personal name to most of them, and we could do the same to many.

We are not unacquainted with Mr Byends of the town of Fair Speech, who "always has the luck to jump in his judgment with the way of the times, and to get thereby," who is zealous for Religion "when he goes in his silver slippers," and "loves to walk with him in the streets when the sun shines and the people applaud him." All his kindred and surroundings are only too familiar to us—his wife, that very virtuous woman my Lady Feigning's daughter, my Lord Fair-speech, my Lord Time-server, Mr. Facingbothways, Mr. Anything, and the Parson of the Parish, his mother's own brother by the father's side, Mr. Twotongues. Nor is his schoolmaster, one Mr. Gripeman, of the market town of Lovegain, in the county of Coveting, a stranger to us. Obstinate, with his dogged determination and stubborn common-sense, and Pliable with his shallow impressionableness, are among our acquaintances.

We have, before now, come across "the brisk lad Ignorance from the town of Conceit," and have made acquaintance with Mercy's would-be suitor, Mr. Brisk, "a man of some breeding and that pretended to religion, but who stuck very close to the world." The man Temporary who lived in a town two miles off from Honesty, and next door to Mr. Turnback; Formalist and Hypocrisy, who were "from the land of Vainglory, and were going for praise to Mount Sion"; Simple, Sloth, and Presumption, "fast asleep by the roadside with fetters on their heels," and their companions, Shortwind, Noheart, Lingerafterlust, and Sleepyhead, we know them all. "The young woman whose name was Dull" taxes our patience every day. Where is the town which does not contain Mrs. Timorous and her coterie of gossips, Mrs. Bats-eyes, Mrs. Inconsiderate, Mrs. Lightmind, and Mrs. Knownothing, "all as merry as the maids," with that pretty fellow Mr. Lechery at the house of Madam Wanton, that "admirably well-bred gentlewoman"?

Where shall we find more lifelike portraits than those of Madam Bubble, a "tall, comely dame, somewhat of a swarthy complexion, speaking very smoothly with a smile at the end of each sentence, wearing a great purse by her side, with her hand often in it, fingering her money as if that was her chief delight;" of poor Feeblemind of the town of Uncertain, with his "whitely look, the cast in his eye, and his trembling speech;" of Littlefaith, as "white as a clout," neither able to fight nor fly when the thieves from Dead Man's Lane were on him; of Ready-to-halt, at first coming along on his crutches, and then when Giant Despair had been slain and Doubting Castle demolished, taking Despondency's daughter Much-afraid by the hand and dancing with her in the road? "True, he could not dance without one crutch in his hand, but I promise you he footed it well. Also the girl was to be commanded, for she answered the musick handsomely." In Bunyan's pictures there is never a superfluous detail. Every stroke tells, and helps to the completeness of the portraiture.

The same reality characterizes the descriptive part of "The Pilgrim's Progress." As his characters are such as he must meet with every day in his native town, so also the scenery and surroundings of his allegory are part of his own everyday life, and reproduce what he had been brought up amidst in his native county, or had noticed in his tinker's wanderings. "Born and bred," writes Kingsley, "in the monotonous Midland, he had no natural images beyond the pastures and brooks, the town and country houses, he saw about him."

The Slough of Despond, with its treacherous quagmire in the midst of the plain, into which a wayfarer might heedlessly fall, with its stepping-stones half drowned in mire; Byepathmeadow, promising so fair, with its stile and footpath on the other side of the fence; the pleasant river fringed with meadows, green all the year long and overshadowed with trees; the thicket all overgrown with briars and thorns, where one tumbled over a bush, another stuck fast in the dirt, some lost their shoes in the mire, and others were fastened from behind with the brambles; the high wall by the roadside over which the fruit trees shot their boughs and tempted the boys with their unripe plums; the arbour with its settle tempting the footsore traveller to drowsiness; the refreshing spring at the bottom of Hill Difficulty; all are evidently drawn from his own experience. Bunyan, in his long tramps, had seen them all. He had known what it was to be in danger of falling into a pit and being dashed to pieces with Vain Confidence, of being drowned in the flooded meadows with Christian and Hopeful; of sinking in deep water when swimming over a river, going down and rising up half dead, and needing all his companion's strength and skill to keep his head above the stream. Vanity Fair is evidently drawn from the life.

The great yearly fair of Stourbridge, close to Cambridge, which Bunyan had probably often visited in his tinker days, with its streets of booths filled with "wares of all kinds from all countries," its "shows, jugglings, cheats games, plays, fools, apes, knaves, and rogues, and that of every kind," its "great one of the fair," its court of justice and power of judgment, furnished him with the materials for his picture. Scenes like these he draws with sharp defined outlines. When he had to describe what he only knew by hearsay, his pictures are shadowy and cold. Never having been very far from home, he had had no experience of the higher types of beauty and grandeur in nature, and his pen moves in fetters when he attempts to describe them. When his pilgrims come to the Hill Difficulty and the Delectable Mountains, the difference is at once seen. All his nobler imagery is drawn from Scripture. As Hallam has remarked, "There is scarcely a circumstance or metaphor in the Old Testament which does not find a place bodily and literally in 'The Pilgrim's Progress,' and this has made his imagination appear more creative than it really is."

It would but weary the reader to follow the details of a narrative which is so universally known. Who needs to be told that in the pilgrimage here described is represented in allegorical dress the course of a human soul convinced of sin, struggling onwards to salvation through the trials and temptations that beset its path to its eternal home? The book is so completely wrought into the mind and memory, that most of us can at once recall the incidents which chequer the pilgrim's way, and realize their meaning; the Slough of Despond, in which the man convinced of his guilt and fleeing from the wrath to come, in his agonizing self-consciousness is in danger of being swallowed up in despair; the Wicket Gate, by which he enters on the strait and narrow way of holiness; the Interpreter's House, with his visions and acted parables; the Wayside Cross, at the sight of which the burden of guilt falls from the pilgrim's back, and he is clothed with change of raiment; the Hill Difficulty, which stands right in his way, and which he must surmount, not circumvent; the lions which he has to pass, not knowing that they are chained; the Palace Beautiful, where he is admitted to the communion of the faithful, and sits down to meat with them.

The Valley of Humiliation, the scene of his desperate but victorious encounter with Apollyon; the Valley of the Shadow of Death, with its evil sights and doleful sounds, where one of the wicked ones whispers into his ear thoughts of blasphemy which he cannot distinguish from the suggestions of his own mind; the cave at the valley's mouth, in which, Giant Pagan having been dead this many a day, his brother, Giant Pope, now sits alone, grinning at pilgrims as they pass by, and biting his nails because he cannot get at them; Vanity Fair, the picture of the world, as St. John describes it, hating the light that puts to shame its own self-chosen darkness, and putting it out if it can, where the Pilgrim's fellow, Faithful, seals his testimony with his death, and the Pilgrim himself barely escapes; the "delicate plain" called Ease, and the little hill, Lucre, where Demas stood "gentlemanlike," to invite the passersby to come and dig in his silver mine; Byepath Meadow, into which the Pilgrim and his newly-found companion stray, and are made prisoners by Giant Despair and shut up in the dungeons of Doubting Castle, and break out of prison by the help of the Key of Promise.

The Delectable Mountains in Immanuel's Land, with their friendly shepherds and the cheering prospect of the far-off heavenly city; the Enchanted Land, with its temptations to spiritual drowsiness at the very end of the journey; the Land of Beulah, the ante-chamber of the city to which they were bound; and, last stage of all, the deep dark river, without a bridge, which had to be crossed before the city was entered; the entrance into its heavenly gates, the pilgrim's joyous reception with all the bells in the city ringing again for joy; the Dreamer's glimpse of its glories through the opened portals—is not every stage of the journey, every scene of the pilgrimage, indelibly printed on our memories, for our warning, our instruction, our encouragement in the race we, as much as they, have each one to run? Have we not all, again and again, shared the Dreamer's feelings—"After that they shut up the Gates; which, when I had seen, I wished myself among them," and prayed, God helping us, that our "dangerous journey"—ever the most dangerous when we see its dangers the least—might end in our "safe arrival at the desired country"?

"The Pilgrim's Progress" exhibits Bunyan in the character by which he would have most desired to be remembered, as one of the most influential of Christian preachers. Hallam, however, claims for him another distinction which would have greatly startled and probably shocked him, as the father of our English novelists. As an allegorist Bunyan had many predecessors, not a few of whom, dating from early times, had taken the natural allegory of the pilgrimage of human life as the basis of their works. But as a novelist he had no one to show him the way. Bunyan was the first to break ground in a field which has since then been so overabundantly worked that the soil has almost lost its productiveness; while few novels written purely with the object of entertainment have ever proved so universally entertaining. Intensely religious as it is in purpose, "The Pilgrim's Progress" may be safely styled the first English novel. "The claim to be the father of English romance," writes Dr. Allon, "which has been sometimes preferred for Defoe, really pertains to Bunyan.

Defoe may claim the parentage of a species, but Bunyan is the creator of the genus." As the parent of fictitious biography it is that Bunyan has charmed the world. On its vivid interest as a story, its universal interest and lasting vitality rest. "Other allegorises," writes Lord Macaulay, "have shown great ingenuity, but no other allegorist has ever been able to touch the heart, and to make its abstractions objects of terror, of pity, and of love." Whatever its deficiencies, literary and religious, may be; if we find incongruities in the narrative, and are not insensible to some grave theological deficiencies; if we are unable without qualification to accept Coleridge's dictum that it is "incomparably the best 'Summa Theologiæ Evangelicæ' ever produced by a writer not miraculously inspired;" even if, with Hallam, we consider its "excellencies great indeed, but not of the highest order," and deem it "a little over-praised," the fact of its universal popularity with readers of all classes and of all orders of intellect remains, and gives this book a unique distinction.

"I have," says Dr. Arnold, when reading it after a long interval, "always been struck by its piety. I am now struck equally or even more by its profound wisdom. It seems to be a complete reflexion of Scripture." And to turn to a critic of very different character, Dean Swift: "I have been better entertained and more improved," writes that cynical pessimist, "by a few pages of this book than by a long discourse on the will and intellect." The favourite of our childhood, as "the most perfect and complex of fairy tales, so human and intelligible," read, as Hallam says, "at an age when the spiritual meaning is either little perceived or little regarded," the "Pilgrim's Progress" becomes the chosen companion of our later years, perused with ever fresh appreciation of its teaching, and enjoyment of its native genius; "the interpreter of life to all who are perplexed with its problems, and the practical guide and solace of all who need counsel and sympathy."

The secret of this universal acceptableness of "The Pilgrim's Progress" lies in the breadth of its religious sympathies. Rigid Puritan as Bunyan was, no book is more completely free from sectarian narrowness. Its reach is as wide as Christianity itself, and it takes hold of every human heart because it is so intensely human. No apology is needed for presenting Mr. Froude's eloquent panegyric: "The Pilgrim, though in Puritan dress, is a genuine man. His experience is so truly human experience that Christians of every persuasion can identify themselves with him; and even those who regard Christianity itself as but a natural outgrowth of the conscience and intellect, and yet desire to live nobly and make the best of themselves, can recognize familiar footprints in every step of Christian's journey.

Thus 'The Pilgrim's Progress' is a book which when once read can never be forgotten. We too, every one of us, are pilgrims on the same road; and images and illustrations come back to us from so faithful an itinerary, as we encounter similar trials, and learn for ourselves the accuracy with which Bunyan has described them. Time cannot impair its interest, or intellectual progress make it cease to be true to experience." Dr. Brown's appreciative words may be added: "With deepest pathos it enters into the stern battle so real to all of us, into those heart-experiences which make up, for all, the discipline of life. It is this especially which has given to it the mighty hold which it has always had upon the toiling poor, and made it the one book above all books well-thumbed and torn to tatters among them. And it is this which makes it one of the first books translated by the missionary who seeks to give true thoughts of God and life to heathen men."

The Second Part of "The Pilgrim's Progress" partakes of the character of almost all continuations. It is, in Mr. Froude's words, "only a feeble reverberation of the first part, which has given it a popularity it would have hardly attained by its own merits. Christiana and her children are tolerated for the pilgrim's sake to whom they belong." Bunyan seems not to have been insensible of this himself, when in his metrical preface he thus introduces his new work:

> Go now my little book to every place
> Where my first Pilgrim has but shown his face.
> Call at their door; if any say 'Who's there?'
> Then answer thus, 'Christiana is here.'
> If they bid thee come in, then enter thou
> With all thy boys. And then, as thou know'st how,
> Tell who they are, also from whence they came;
> Perhaps they'll know them by their looks or name.

But although the Second Part must be pronounced inferior, on the whole, to the first, it is a work of striking individuality and graphic power, such as Bunyan alone could have written. Everywhere we find strokes of his peculiar genius, and though in a smaller measure than the first, it has added not a few portraits to Bunyan's spiritual picture gallery we should be sorry to miss, and supplied us with racy sayings which stick to the memory. The sweet maid Mercy affords a lovely picture of gentle feminine piety, well contrasted with the more vigorous but still thoroughly womanly character of Christiana.

Great-Heart is too much of an abstraction: a preacher in the uncongenial disguise of a knightly champion of distressed females and the slayer of giants. But the other new characters have generally a vivid personality. Who can forget Old Honesty, the dull good man with no mental gifts but of dogged sincerity, who though coming from the

Town of Stupidity, four degrees beyond the City of Destruction, was "known for a cock of the right kind," because he said the truth and stuck to it; or his companion, Mr. Fearing, that most troublesome of pilgrims, stumbling at every straw, lying roaring at the Slough of Despond above a month together, standing shaking and shrinking at the Wicket Gate, but making no stick at the Lions, and at last getting over the river not much above wetshod; or Mr. Valiant for Truth, the native of Darkland, standing with his sword drawn and his face all bloody from his three hours' fight with Wildhead, Inconsiderate, and Pragmatick.

Mr. Standfast, blushing to be found on his knees in the Enchanted Ground, one who loved to hear his Lord spoken of, and coveted to set his foot wherever he saw the print of his shoe; Mr. Feeblemind, the sickly, melancholy pilgrim, at whose door death did usually knock once a day, betaking himself to a pilgrim's life because he was never well at home, resolved to run when he could, and go when he could not run, and creep when he could not go, an enemy to laughter and to gay attire, bringing up the rear of the company with Mr. Readytohalt hobbling along on his crutches; Giant Despair's prisoners, Mr. Despondency, whom he had all but starved to death—and Mistress Much-afraid his daughter, who went through the river singing, though none could understand what she said? Each of these characters has a distinct individuality which lifts them from shadowy abstractions into living men and women.

But with all its excellencies, and they are many, the general inferiority of the history of Christiana and her children's pilgrimage to that of her husband's must be acknowledged. The story is less skilfully constructed; the interest is sometimes allowed to flag; the dialogues that interrupt the narrative are in places dry and wearisome—too much of sermons in disguise. There is also a want of keeping between the two parts of the allegory. The Wicket Gate of the First Part has become a considerable building with a summer parlour in the Second; the shepherds' tents on the Delectable Mountains have risen into a palace, with a dining-room, and a looking-glass, and a store of jewels; while Vanity Fair has lost its former bad character, and has become a respectable country town, where Christiana and her family, seeming altogether to forget their pilgrimage, settled down comfortably, enjoy the society of the good people of the place, and the sons marry and have children.

These same children also cause the reader no little perplexity, when he finds them in the course of the supposed journey transformed from sweet babes who are terrified with the Mastiffs barking at the Wicket Gate, who catch at the boughs for the unripe plums and cry at having to climb the hill; whose faces are stroked by the Interpreter; who are catechised and called "good boys" by Prudence; who sup on bread crumbled into basins of milk, and are put to bed by Mercy—into strong young men, able to go out and fight with a giant, and lend a hand to the pulling down of Doubting Castle, and becoming husbands and fathers. We cannot but feel the want of vraisemblance which brings the whole company of pilgrims to the banks of the dark river at one time, and sends them over in succession, following one another rapidly through the Golden Gate of the City. The four boys with their wives and children, it is true, stay behind awhile, but there is an evident incongruity in their doing so when the allegory has brought them all to what stands for the close of their earthly pilgrimage. Bunyan's mistake was in gratifying his inventive genius and making his band of pilgrims so large. He could get them together and make them travel in company without any sacrifice of dramatic truth, which, however, he was forced to disregard when the time came for their dismissal.

The exquisite pathos of the description of the passage of the river by Christian and Hopeful blinds us to what may be almost termed the impossibility of two persons passing through the final struggle together, and dying at the same moment, but this charm is wanting in the prosaic picture of the company of fellow-travellers coming down to the water's edge, and waiting till the postman blows his horn and bids them cross. Much as the Second Part contains of what is admirable, and what no one but Bunyan could have written, we feel after reading it that, in Mr. Froude's words, the rough simplicity is gone, and has been replaced by a tone of sentiment which is almost mawkish. "Giants, dragons, and angelic champions carry us into a spurious fairyland where the knight-errant is a preacher in disguise. Fair ladies and love-matches, however decorously chastened, suit ill with the sternness of the mortal conflict between the soul and sin." With the acknowledged shortcomings of the Second Part of "The Pilgrim's Progress," we may be well content that Bunyan never carried out the idea hinted at in the closing words of his allegory: "Shall it be my lot to go that way again, I may give those that desire it an account of what I am here silent about; in the meantime I bid my reader—Adieu."

Bunyan's second great allegorical work, "The Holy War," need not detain us long. Being an attempt, and in the nature of things an unsuccessful attempt, to clothe what writers on divinity call "the plan of salvation" in a figurative dress, the narrative, with all its vividness of description in parts, its clearly drawn characters with their picturesque nomenclature, and the stirring vicissitudes of the drama, is necessarily wanting in the personal interest which attaches to an individual man, like Christian, and those who are linked with or follow his career.

In fact, the tremendous realities of the spiritual history of the human race are entirely unfit for allegorical treatment as a whole. Sin, its origin, its consequences, its remedy, and the apparent failure of that remedy though administered by Almighty hands, must remain a mystery for all time. The attempts made by Bunyan, and by one of much higher intellectual power and greater poetic gifts than Bunyan—John Milton—to bring that mystery within the grasp of the finite intellect, only render it more perplexing. The proverbial line tells us that—

Fools rush in where angels fear to tread.

Bunyan and Milton were as far as possible from being "fools"; but when both these great writers, on the one hand, carry us up into the Council Chamber of Heaven and introduce us to the Persons of the ever-blessed Trinity, debating, consulting, planning, and resolving, like a sovereign and his ministers when a revolted province has to be brought back to its allegiance; and, on the other hand, take us down to the infernal regions, and makes us privy to the plots and counterplots of the rebel leaders and hearers of their speeches, we cannot but feel that, in spite of the magnificent diction and poetic imagination of the one, and the homely picturesque genius of the other, the grand themes treated of are degraded if not vulgarized, without our being in any way helped to unravel their essential mysteries.

In point of individual personal interest, "The Holy War" contrasts badly with "The Pilgrim's Progress." The narrative moves in a more shadowy region. We may admire the workmanship; but the same undefined sense of unreality pursues us through Milton's noble epic, the outcome of a divinely-fired genius, and Bunyan's humble narrative, drawing its scenes and circumstances, and to some extent its dramatis personæ, from the writer's own surroundings in the town and corporation of Bedford, and his brief but stirring experience as a soldier in the great Parliamentary War. The catastrophe also is eminently unsatisfactory.

When Christian and Hopeful enter the Golden Gates we feel that the story has come to its proper end, which we have been looking for all along. But the conclusion of "The Holy War" is too much like the closing chapter of "Rasselas"—"a conclusion in which nothing is concluded." After all the endless vicissitudes of the conflict, and the final and glorious victory of Emmanuel and his forces, and the execution of the ringleaders of the mutiny, the issue still remains doubtful. The town of Mansoul is left open to fresh attacks. Diabolus is still at large. Carnal Sense breaks prison and continues to lurk in the town. Unbelief, that "nimble Jack," slips away, and can never be laid hold of. These, therefore, and some few others of the more subtle of the Diabolonians, continue to make their home in Mansoul, and will do so until Mansoul ceases to dwell in the kingdom of Universe.

It is true they turn chicken-hearted after the other leaders of their party have been taken and executed, and keep themselves quiet and close, lurking in dens and holes lest they should be snapped up by Emmanuel's men. If Unbelief or any of his crew venture to show themselves in the streets, the whole town is up in arms against them; the very children raise a hue and cry against them and seek to stone them. But all in vain. Mansoul, it is true, enjoys some good degree of peace and quiet. Her Prince takes up his residence in her borders. Her captains and soldiers do their duties. She minds her trade with the heavenly land afar off; also she is busy in her manufacture. But with the remnants of the Diabolonians still within her walls, ready to show their heads on the least relaxation of strict watchfulness, keeping up constant communication with Diabolus and the other lords of the pit, and prepared to open the gates to them when opportunity offers, this peace can not be lasting.

The old battle will have to be fought over again, only to end in the same undecisive result. And so it must be to the end. If untrue to art, Bunyan is true to fact. Whether we regard Mansoul as the soul of a single individual or as the whole human race, no final victory can be looked for so long as it abides in "the country of Universe." The flesh will lust against the spirit, the regenerated man will be in danger of being brought into captivity to the law of sin and death unless he keeps up his watchfulness and maintains the struggle to the end.

And it is here, that, for purposes of art, not for purposes of truth, the real failing of "The Holy War" lies. The drama of Mansoul is incomplete, and whether individually or collectively, must remain incomplete till man puts on a new nature, and the victory, once for all gained on Calvary, is consummated, in the fulness of time, at the restitution of all things. There is no uncertainty what the end will be. Evil must be put down, and good must triumph at last. But the end is not yet, and it seems as far off as ever.

The army of Doubters, under their several captains, Election Doubters, Vocation Doubters, Salvation Doubters, Grace Doubters, with their general the great Lord Incredulity at their head, reinforced by many fresh regiments under novel standards, unknown and unthought of in Bunyan's days, taking the place of those whose power is past, is ever making new attacks upon poor Mansoul, and terrifying feeble souls with their threatenings. Whichever way we look there is much to puzzle, much to grieve over, much that to our present limited view is entirely inexplicable. But the mind that accepts the loving will and wisdom of God as the law of the Universe, can rest in the calm assurance that all, however mysteriously, is fulfilling His eternal designs, and that though He seems to permit "His work to be spoilt, His power defied, and even His victories when won made useless," it is but seeming,—that the triumph of evil is but temporary, and that these apparent failures and contradictions, are slowly but surely working out and helping forward

The one unseen divine event
To which the whole creation moves.

"The mysteries and contradictions which the Christian revelation leaves unsolved are made tolerable by Hope." To adopt Bunyan's figurative language in the closing paragraph of his allegory, the day is certainly coming when the famous town of Mansoul shall be taken down and transported "every stick and stone" to Emmanuel's land, and there set up for the Father's habitation in such strength and glory as it never saw before. No Diabolonian shall be able to creep into its streets, burrow in its walls, or be seen in its borders. No evil tidings shall trouble its inhabitants, nor sound of Diabolian drum be heard there. Sorrow and grief shall be ended, and life, always sweet, always new, shall last longer than they could even desire it, even all the days of eternity. Meanwhile let those who have such a glorious hope set before them keep clean and white the liveries their Lord has given them, and wash often in the open fountain. Let them believe in His love, live upon His word; watch, fight, and pray, and hold fast till He come.

One more work of Bunyan's still remains to be briefly noticed, as bearing the characteristic stamp of his genius, "The Life and Death of Mr. Badman." The original idea of this book was to furnish a contrast to "The Pilgrim's Progress." As in that work he had described the course of a man setting out on his course heavenwards, struggling onwards through temptation, trials, and difficulties, and entering at last through the golden gates into the city of God, so in this later work his purpose was to depict the career of a man whose face from the first was turned in the opposite direction, going on from bad to worse, ever becoming more and more irretrievably evil, fitter and fitter for the bottomless pit; his life full of sin and his death without repentance; reaping the fruit of his sins in hopeless sinfulness.

That this was the original purpose of the work, Bunyan tells us in his preface. It came into his mind, he says, as in the former book he had written concerning the progress of the Pilgrim from this world to glory, so in this second book to write of the life and death of the ungodly, and of their travel from this world to hell. The new work, however, as in almost every respect it differs from the earlier one, so it is decidedly inferior to it. It is totally unlike "The Pilgrim's Progress" both in form and execution. The one is an allegory, the other a tale, describing without imagery or metaphor, in the plainest language, the career of a "vulgar, middle-class, unprincipled scoundrel." While "The Pilgrim's Progress" pursues the narrative form throughout, only interrupted by dialogues between the leading characters, "Mr. Badman's career" is presented to the world in a dialogue between a certain Mr. Wiseman and Mr. Attentive. Mr. Wiseman tells the story, and Mr. Attentive supplies appropriate reflections on it.

The narrative is needlessly burdened with a succession of short sermons, in the form of didactic discourses on lying, stealing, impurity, and the other vices of which the hero of the story was guilty, and which brought him to his miserable end. The plainness of speech with which some of these evil doings are enlarged upon, and Mr. Badman's indulgence in them described, makes portions of the book very disagreeable, and indeed hardly profitable reading. With omissions, however, the book well deserves perusal, as a picture such as only Bunyan or his rival in lifelike portraiture, Defoe, could have drawn of vulgar

English life in the latter part of the seventeenth century, in a commonplace country town such as Bedford. It is not at all a pleasant picture. The life described, when not gross, is sordid and foul, is mean and commonplace.

But as a description of English middle-class life at the epoch of the Restoration and Revolution, it is invaluable for those who wish to put themselves in touch with that period. The anecdotes introduced to illustrate Bunyan's positions of God's judgment upon swearers and sinners, convicting him of a credulity and a harshness of feeling one is sorry to think him capable of, are very interesting for the side-lights they throw upon the times and the people who lived in them. It would take too long to give a sketch of the story, even if a summary could give any real estimate of its picturesque and vivid power. It is certainly a remarkable, if an offensive book.

As with "Robinson Crusoe" and Defoe's other tales, we can hardly believe that we have not a real history before us. We feel that there is no reason why the events recorded should not have happened. There are no surprises; no unlooked-for catastrophes; no providential interpositions to punish the sinner or rescue the good man. Badman's pious wife is made to pay the penalty of allowing herself to be deceived by a tall, good-looking, hypocritical scoundrel. He himself pursues his evil way to the end, and "dies like a lamb, or as men call it, like a Chrisom child sweetly and without fear," but the selfsame Mr. Badman still, not only in name, but in condition; sinning onto the last, and dying with a heart that cannot repent.

Mr. Froude's summing up of this book is so masterly that we make no apology for presenting it to our readers. "Bunyan conceals nothing, assumes nothing, and exaggerates nothing. He makes his bad man sharp and shrewd. He allows sharpness and shrewdness to bring him the reward which such qualities in fact command. Badman is successful; is powerful; he enjoys all the pleasures which money can bring; his bad wife helps him to ruin, but otherwise he is not unhappy, and he dies in peace. Bunyan has made him a brute, because such men do become brutes. It is the real punishment of brutal and selfish habits. There the figure stands—a picture of a man in the rank of English life with which Bunyan was most familiar; travelling along the primrose path to the everlasting bonfire, as the way to Emmanuel's Land was through the Slough of Despond and the Valley of the Shadow of Death. Pleasures are to be found among the primroses, such pleasures as a brute can be gratified by. Yet the reader feels that even if there was no bonfire, he would still prefer to be with Christian."

ABOUT JOHN BUNYAN

John Bunyan, the famous religious author who wrote *The Pilgrim's Progress*, was born in the town of Elstow in England in 1628. He was the son of a traveling tinker who created and sold kitchen tools and other useful items.

Bunyan's career as an author was heavily influenced by reading the popular tales of the day, which were usually about adventures of honorable knights and spurious knaves. These fanciful stories were sold at the fair in Cambridge, which would someday be the inspiration for the Vanity Fair in Bunyan's most famous work, *The Pilgrim's Progress*. He also became familiar with other literature that was popular for Puritans of the day to read, such as *Foxe's Book of Martyrs*, and various moral dialogues and religious homilies. But most importantly, John spent a lot of time studying an authorized version of the English Bible when he was just twelve years old.

In 1644 several tragedies occurred that changed young Bunyan's life forever. His mom died in June, and his sister died a short few months later. In August, his father married again for the third time. At the same time, the English Civil Wars were ongoing, and John was sent to assist the garrison at a small town in Buckinghamshire called Newport Pagnell. The garrison's leader was governor Sir Samuel Luke, an ardent Presbyterian. Bunyan worked at Newport for three years, and most likely did not engage in armed conflict.

Soon after being released from the military in July of 1647, Bunyan married to a woman named Mary. Both him and his wife were extremely poor. He says in his autobiography that they "came together as poor as poor might be, not having so much household-stuff as a dish or spoon betwixt us both."

However, Bunyan's wife did bring two books with her that she had inherited from her religious-minded father. The books were *Practice of Piety* by Lewis Bayly and *The Plain Man's Pathway to Heaven* by Arthur Dent. Both of these classics helped to shape Bunyan's religious views.

Bunyan and his wife had four children together. A little blind girl, Mary, named after her mother, was baptized in 1650. Elizabeth, John, and Thomas were added to the family before John's wife died in 1658.

Before John Bunyan became a famous religious author, he had to go through a spiritual struggle that was very painful and personal. This slow but gradual conversion to Puritanism lasted for a whole decade, and started shortly after his first marriage.

First, Bunyan went through a cycle of conformity to Anglican values, in which he grudgingly went to church and gave up many of his favorite recreational activities. Dancing, bell ringing, and sports were some of the pastimes that were put aside. Then came an agonizing focus on his inner spiritual life. At times, the mental torture almost seemed physical. John would later describe the "storms of temptation", the scripture verses which threatened damnation, pinching his soul and making him very sore.

Finally, one morning Bunyan had had enough, and fell on his knees and gave everything to Christ. The discouraging voices of Satan were rebuked and sent away. He described this moment by writing "down I fell as a bird that is shot from the tree." Bunyan grew greatly in his spiritual walk when he joined the Bedford Separatist church in 1655 and became friends with its fiery leader, John Gifford.

The Bedford community church was an open-communion facility, accepting anyone who believed "faith in Christ and holiness of life." They also practiced a more modern style of baptism, believing that only adults should be baptized, and that they should be fully immersed. Bunyan embraced the Bedford church and soon became a lay preacher.

As he had recently conquered his own personal demons, Bunyan was fitted to help console and warn other members.

Bunyan had a strong passion for sharing the gospel, and soon he became known as a fiery preacher. He wrote: "I went myself in Chains to preach to them in Chains, and carried that Fire in my own Conscience that I persuaded them to beware of." While he did spend part of his ministry visiting fellow church members, much of Bunyan's time was spent publicly debating Quaker opponents in the markets of Bedfordshire and other small towns. He also wrote his first books during this time, including *Some Gospel Truths Opened*.

In 1660, a period of change took place in England. The Irish, Scottish, and English monarchies were all united under King Charles II. This ended the religious peace and freedom that churches had enjoyed for nearly 20 years.

Despite the change in the political climate, John Bunyan refused to change his actions. On November 12, 1660, he was seized and brought before a local judge, who charged him with holding a church service that was not in conformity with state church of England. Bunyan refused to assure the magistrate that he would not stop holding religious services, and he was promptly thrown in jail, where he was kept for the next 12 years.

Even though he was imprisoned, Bunyan's conditions were lenient. He was allowed to make and sell "long Tagg'd laces" to help support his family. He was also allowed to be let out at times to visit family and friends, and to speak at meetings. But most importantly, Bunyan was able to write, starting with his autobiography, *Grace Abounding*, in 1666. During this time, he also started work on *Pilgrim's Progress*, but didn't finish it until a year after being released from prison in 1678.

Bunyan's greatest work, The Pilgrim's Progress, was very popular. It is considered one of the last great works in the folksy tradition of the regular, common people.

ABOUT JOHN BUNYAN

The popularity of Bunyan's books led to a busy preaching schedule. While keeping up with tending to the Bedford church, he also traveled to London frequently to preach in Congregational churches.

Despite his newfound popularity as a speaker, Bunyan was able to keep up his career as a writer. He wrote a several more allegories, and also authored a book of poems for children. After a preaching visit in 166, Bunyan died and was buried in Bunhill Fields, which was a traditional graveyard for non-conformists.

Despite the ongoing civil wars and conflict over his lifetime, Bunyan wrote several religious classics, and is today regarded as one of the greatest Christian authors.

www.ingramcontent.com/pod-product-compliance
Lightning Source LLC
Chambersburg PA
CBHW070106080526
44586CB00013B/1204